Justice is God's Idea

Justice is God's Idea

Man Has Corrupted and Destroyed It!

Frank Walters

authorHOUSE®

AuthorHouse™
1663 Liberty Drive
Bloomington, IN 47403
www.authorhouse.com
Phone: 1-800-839-8640

Published by AuthorHouse   1/5/2012

ISBN: 978-1-4634-3497-7 (sc)
ISBN: 978-1-4634-3496-0 (dj)
ISBN: 978-1-4634-3495-3 (ebk)

Library of Congress Control Number: 2011912502

CONTENTS

Preface.. ix
Corruption with a Capital "C" 1
It wasn't always this way 4
The 70's—A Man takes A Badge... 10
Exams are for dummies and Stealing Time 15
Badges for Sale 21
Unequal Justice for All 25
The Wizard of Court House Corruption.. 36
The Case of Officer "T"-the whistleblower who wasn't........................ 40
When No meant no job—The case of "G" 51
Are There Any Decent Ones Left? 58
The Mighty Have Fallen 72
The structure of the courts and how they function 79
The state of the Court System Today... 82

Acknowledgements

This book is dedicated to my mother and father who worked tirelessly to make my life just a bit easier. For their morals and their ethics, I salute you. Also with much love to my children and grandchildren who give me love and support every day in every way. Poppa loves you.

"Justice has nothing to do with what goes on in a courtroom Justice is what comes out of a courtroom."
Clarence Darrow

Preface

This book is dedicated to the men and women who honorably serve in the court systems in and around the United States today. From the secretaries to the judges, there are no easy jobs.

For every day, haunted souls flood the courtrooms and hallways seeking justice.

To the officers who stand guard; the stenographers who memorialize the events and the clerks who keep things moving; this is a testimony.

We know how things should be done—the problem is huge and it must be addressed.

When there is any sort of tragedy there is always collateral damage. When someone is convicted of a crime or loses a prestigious job or even a job they've had for a decade or two, people get hurt. Those that are in the background, the children and the family members are innocent of any wrongdoing, but sometimes their suffering is even greater. They stand by in the wreckage and try to piece their lives back together

For this reason, no actual names have been used. Instead, you will read initials, or nicknames in some cases no names at all; this is highly intentional.

As a Court Officer, I took an oath to serve and protect; some habits especially old ones; die hard.

This book begins with the start of my career in the Court System. This is mainly so that the reader may know that it wasn't always like this and it doesn't have to be like this. It also serves to show you that I learned the Court system in every aspect; as I was very young when first employed. These observations and comments come from many years of hard learned experience.

The Court system has changed radically through these many decades and probably not for the better. The buildings of course have not changed. They are the same alabaster and granite that were erected more than fifty years ago.

But since the time of World War II and the fly boys, the GI Bill and nightly radio; everything else has changed.

Paranoia is everywhere, more so than when Senator Joe McCarthy was hunting Communists in the fifties. This is probably because the corruption has touched so many people that many well-meaning individuals who would never think of wrong doing in any other circumstance; are up to their eyeballs and surrounded by-corruption.

Every depiction of events is drawn from the actual event as they happened. No license has been taken except when necessary to protect the innocent or for those who still work in the system and would be the object of derision and scorn; most likely much worse, were it thought that they contributed to this work.

The internet is jammed with websites about legal, political and courtroom corruption. In fact, there is a movement afoot to amend the Constitution to include the political corruption of public servants and proper punishment. These well-meaning pundits are fine in their intent but, they lack the inside knowledge and mechanical insight that grows out of working in the system for more than half of one's life.

You will conclude that the Court system is in need of a massive reform. It is my theory that the support staff and officers learned to lie, cheat and steal by example. As Alan Dershowitz wrote in his book "The Best Defense", "lying, distortion and other forms of intellectual dishonesty are endemic among judges . . . . I have seen corruption, incompetence, bias, laziness, meanness of spirit, and plain ordinary stupidity"

Did these clowns learn at the feet of the Masters or is it the environment that produces the evil itself? Is it when people's lives are on the line every day that we become hardened like the criminals who wander the halls and inhabit the cells?

Is it then that anarchy will reign and the barbarians will surely overtake the gates.

We must do what we can if it is only by awareness to end the corruption. Now!

"Our Country is now taking so steady
a course as to show by what road
it will pass to destruction, to wit;
by consolidation of power first,
and then corruption, its necessary
consequence."
Thomas Jefferson

Corruption with a Capital "C"

"Justice, Justice, thou shalt pursue." Deuteronomy 16:20.

The name of the game is corruption and the court system is filled with it. I am not talking about petty payoffs or smearing somebody for a courtesy. I am talking about putrid, scandalous behavior that one would expect to find in a back alley brawl or from competing used car salesmen.

As in any criminal enterprise, someone is always in charge. In our Court House, the one I retired from it was a Major, not the Administrative Judge and not the Chief of the Officers or the Chief Clerk. This certain Major, for there was more than one among us he was special; very special—let's call him what he was—a henchman, who controlled a gang of officers as well.

The best name that I could devise for him, with a "g" rating, of course is the Wizard of Court House Corruption. This is because so many things happened around him, the good and the not so good, as if by magic.

He was so good at his game that he could even make people lose their jobs and disappear. Being dissed by the Wizard of Court House Corruption had a very different meaning. If he put you in his crosshairs, watch out, he was going to get you. You better consider putting in your papers, for a transfer or retirement, because life would be hell unless you got out of his way.

In one particular circumstance, I ran up against this guy because they were roasting a fellow officer. Now I don't mean like a comedy roast, more like burning at the stake. They were trying and succeeding in stripping him of everything, so of course I tried to intercede. I went to the top Brass

1

and I was told "My hands are tied—he's (the Wizard of Court House Corruption) been put in charge by Judge X, the court *belongs* to him."

Can you imagine? The guy they were referring to was not a judge. Every court is technically administered by a judge. But, to be fair, much more goes on outside of the court rooms than inside and outside in the corridors, public hallways and offices, this guy ruled. He was a Court Officer who no doubt bought his rank.

This was a man who was carrying on an extra marital affair with a married woman that he worked with, which was a major policy infraction, and the affair was going on for more than a decade without even a slap on the wrist. These two had been together so long that they attended functions together as a couple. No one even knew what their spouses looked like!

This character is not immoral. He is amoral. He sells badges; yep you got that right, more on that later. He sells verdicts. He fixes whatever he wants to whenever he feels like for whomever he feels like because he is the Wizard of Court House Corruption and the Court House and its inhabitants are his and his alone. Like a favorite set of trains that he watches go around the track, everyone is under his scrutiny.

The judges walk on eggshells around him. His fellow officers bow and scrape, they laugh at his jokes, and most importantly look the other way, while he turns what should be a pillar of justice into a stinking hole, a cesspool of corruption, graft and swindles.

This is the world that I stepped, or more likely ran out of when I retired. It was a far cry from the one that I entered.

"The duty of the young is to challenge corruption."
Kurt Cobain

It wasn't always this way

I loved the job. It really was my identity. For thirty years I put on a starched and pressed uniform and did what I thought I could to see that justice was served.

Somewhere down the line, though things went horribly wrong.

Well, about a year before I retired, I really started to feel like an inmate surrounded by thugs in uniforms. Don't get me wrong, the atmosphere in the Court House was likened by many to be that of a college frat house. Constant pranks and practical jokes, food being swapped around, people being teased about their hair, their cologne, whatever you could think of on an adolescent level of humor—it went on. It was all good-natured and we considered ourselves like brothers. The most childish and goofy remarks would help lighten the tension.

Don't forget in this Court House we saw it all; from prostitutes to serial killers; from pedophiles to wife beaters. They all passed through our doors and we were the handlers of this sea of human tragedy.

Early in my tenure, I defended a buddy's life. We were physically attacked by five knife-wielding relatives of a convicted felon who was up on new charges in Criminal Court. Their plan was a Bonnie and Clyde sort of breakout and it was well thought out. Were it not for myself and my fellow officer, several people including many civilians could have been killed.

The officer and I actually re-entered the building after leaving unharmed without our uniform shirts. They were able to get the gun of another officer and all hell broke loose. To this day, the injuries I sustained haunt me, and at that time, I was out of work on short term disability for several months.

Because of the bond that we felt for one another, and because I knew what real camaraderie was I believed it could not be compromised, that it could not be blemished. I was wrong.

We had a few court officers in the eighty's that would actually steal traffic tickets that were being processed. They would choose to rip them up to unrecognizable shreds; or fill out the backs, stamp them with a judge's stamp and then sign the judge's name. This was not done ad hoc or just for kicks but for friends, family and business associates. There was one particular offender who was quite busy doing this for a number of folks, and eventually he was caught.

I remember thinking vividly that I knew this was the guy that I wanted to watch my back in case something went horribly wrong. It's bad when you don't know who the bad guy is.

There were thankfully few occasions when things did go badly. One such time, there was a problem in the detention area. This wonderful coward, who had the biggest mouth in the bunch; ran out of the detention area and left myself and another area alone to deal with an inmate fight that just broke out. Rather than serving at his post, he was found in the lunch room.

Before he was an officer of the Court, he was a local Town cop who, when he was called to a crime scene, drew his shotgun and; shot a statue!

But here I was with a lifetime on the job, not at full retirement age but hit so hard in the face with the realization that justice had been bastardized to the point where she was no longer blind, nor fair. It was there for the taking at the right price. I was working in an asylum and the inmates were in charge.

Finding an honest co-worker was like trying to find a virgin in a whorehouse. If the staff were not politically appointed, they were sleeping with someone, incompetent, related to someone or had paid someone off to get their jobs. While this seems like it is a wild rant. It is not, not even an exaggeration. I dreaded going into work; I felt that I could trust no one and everyone around me felt the same way.

The spirit of fraternity and camaraderie was a sham. Although I was not happy with the decision, I knew it was time to go.

The same scenarios kept repeating themselves over and over again. Promotions for a price, fixed exams, disciplinary actions for the unpopular and threats and horrible acts of retaliation and retribution for those who refused to toe the line.

The worst thing was that the Court House is like an ethnic neighborhood. Everyone knows everyone else's business. Who is sleeping with whom, who took a bribe for what verdict; who is Judge So and So's bag man. Worse still; we knew what judges were sex addicts, drug or alcohol dependent, gamblers, just straight thieves, who would take a bribe or throw a trial and rarely who wouldn't and lastly; of course, who was untouchable.

These were the few that served at the behest of the War Lords of the Republican Machine and they could do whatever they wanted to whoever they felt like it. These were the judges on the bench that were so unfit that they went from being teachers to law school right onto the bench.

Another judge was given a ten year judgeship because she and her husband were divorcing. This way, he didn't have to worry about alimony. Oh, yes, I forgot to mention, he is an Executive Leader of the Republican Committee; a bona fide machine member. Every judge would make sure to rule in his favor, so his law practice thrived.

There was a cadre of lawyers who could win any case. In my early days, I didn't understand it, until an older guy clued me in. No different than the record industry, the Court House functioned on Payola. It was sort of a sliding fee scale. The worse the charge the more money they charged.

There were the few judges who were not included in the bribery scheme, but they drove the old cars and didn't own condos on Paradise Island. One guy was so efficient at getting rid of cases via bribery; he got a reputation for being "liberal".

To disguise his actions, he always set a decently high bail, guaranteeing his bribe in a way. He put two kids through college this way.

But, after watching the system that I swore to uphold and defend, be decimated and disrespected on a minute to minute basis, I realized enough was enough. At first I reacted like a macho guy, tried to change some things, make things better for myself and my fellow officers. I stuck up for people when they were ridiculed or singled out unnecessarily.

I was getting worn down like a pebble in the ocean. When I put my uniform on; it wasn't with the same degree of pride. I didn't want to tell people what I did for a living. Rather than being boastful, I was ashamed. It felt like I worked with a bunch of pirates.

Two in particular, a Major, who has a mistress who was also on the job, were relentless in their defilement of the system and their perversion of whatever power they were given. Their lust for power was only matched by their lust for one another.

This was so far away from the guy (me) who worked two jobs to make ends meet and stubbornly refused to quit the Courts because I felt that I was doing good for society.

What good is it when people's lives are ruined and their pensions are ripped away from them like a game of ping pong?

What good is it when people find ways to peddle Officer's badges, what then is the badge really worth?

What good is it when exams for advancement are rigged with a select group of candidates knowing the exam in advance?

This was my workplace when I decided that I could take no more and put in my retirement papers. The following pages detail corruption that is eating a good and fair system away like the most vicious cancer we know.

This corruption is rampant from the rank and file officers to the Judges; no one is exempt. The corruption of the Court system I turned my back on is like a horrible monster with a relentless appetite and it grows bigger and badder by the day.

"Justice consists in doing no injury to men, decency in giving them no offense."
Marcus Tullius Cicero

The 70's—A Man takes A Badge

Life in uniform began for me in my mid-twenties. I was fit and fine. Some say I turned heads. I was a student of martial arts, and could handle myself on the street or in the courtroom.

So, here I was about to become like Wyatt Earp; one of the good guys; ready to fight in the courts of Long Island. I was very excited.

Boy, did I have a lot to learn. You see, I started as a Senior Court Officer.

After a brief time in rank, I was promoted to the position of a Personal Officer.

A Personal Officer is assigned to a single judge, not on a daily or rotational basis like most court assignments; but to that judge exclusively. Now this can be heaven or hell depending on the chemistry between you and your judge; and also how much of a gentleman or lady your judge was. You see some judges viewed this privilege as an additional domestic servant, only at work, while others treated their officers as part of a team and consulted with them and acknowledged and respected them.

My experience with my judge, Judge S was unbelievable. I had my own small office that I worked out of for three years. For all of those three years while at work, I never left his side. He was a judge's judge. He was not soft on crime or on those who committed them. But, when he spoke, you listened for he was wise and knowledgeable.

While he was sentencing two defendants after a difficult trial for a particularly grisly time, he spoke words that went on to be commemorated in film. He sentenced the two men, then in their twenties, to twenty five years to life for the cold blooded murder of a local business owner. One young man spoke up after being sentenced and said "Your Honor, I'm never going to be able to do all that time." The judge said that he regretted that he would not be alive to ensure that they would serve the minimum, and went on to reply to the young man; "Well son, just do the best you can.

I enjoyed going to work with him, it really didn't feel like work, because I learned so much about the law, the system, but most of all how to discriminate between who I could trust and who I could not trust.

I was responsible for the Judge's personal safety and also arranged personal appointments for him determining who had access to him. This was a very heady position for a twenty something to find himself in. I was carrying a gun, as a Court Officer assigned to County Court as this was a criminal venue. Officers in the District Court would wait some years for this privilege.

At one point, I was the range instructor for all of the Court Officers when they started to carry weapons. Weaponry is something that is necessary but I am always reluctant to strap on a gun, the potential for an unstable individual to try and grab a weapon is always there and no one ever wants to see anyone get shot.

Amid the tumultuous times of the 70's, when we thought we had to protect judges one on one; Judge S was a prince.

He treated me so well, like a member of his family. I worried about his safety because he was getting up in years and had put away a lot of bad people. The bad guys never forget the DA or the judge who send them away. They do forget though, that they put themselves behind bars as it is always easier to strike out at someone else than to take responsibility for one's own failings.

Being that close to a judge is like going to law school. Every day you learn something that stretches your mind about legal concepts. At the time that I was in his service, I had two kids with one more on the way, and he still nudged me every once in a while about going to law school.

He made me feel like a million dollars and I gained an immense respect for judges because of him. He was the ideal.

Sadly, he aged out of the system, and I could no longer be in his service. I knew that I would never have another court experience like this. I mention how wonderful he was not only to acknowledge and thank him; although he has long since passed, but also to show the stark contrast between him and some of the shady, shifty characters that inhabit the harrowed halls of justice now.

That is not to say that the majority of judges are bad, I cannot offer an opinion on that. I only know that there are many who live in that grey area between morality and immorality and quite a few of those that do hail from Nassau County, NY.

What I learned on my job with Judge S., I carried with me throughout my Court career. My next assignment as a County Marshal was certainly an eye opener.

My Dad was a Marshal before me. In fact, he was so well thought of on his job, that they dubbed him as the Marshal with a heart. But after all, he was a hero long before he was a Marshal and I learned at his knee.

He was a Republican Committeeman and that rarified air that he breathed with so many powerful cronies allowed him to access this job for me. I had no idea; I just thought that he put in a good word for me, knowing that I had a wife and a handful of young kids to take care of.

But jobs are always hard to come by especially when they come with good medical benefits and pensions, so he did what he had to do. He bought and sold tickets to political functions, he was a loyal and active member of the party.

He helped raise lots of money. This money was used to further a political agenda. He fed the most powerful and efficient political machine in the country to date. Then what do you know? Bingo! Sonny boy had a job.

Why talk of Tammany Hall when we have our own backroom potboilers right here in suburban Long Island. A former party boss, did hard time for raking money in from the faithful. His allies still defend him as doing nothing different than anyone else. The only difference they will tell you is that he got caught. The current boss was intended to be only a placeholder until he got drunk with the power and decided to hold on to it. This present regime is so slick they ooze.

Now, here I was fresh off the experience of having worn civilian clothes for the last three years and basically keeping bankers' hours. Now I was going to serve with an elite corps of highly seasoned men.

By some, they were dubbed the party boss' storm troopers. We were tough and efficient. In the beginning though, for me it was another story.

Of course, I still remember, my first day "on the job". I was handed a badge and a black jack and told to "go be a Marshal". I spent ten years in that capacity. I saw a lot during that time. But nothing I saw could have prepared me for what was to follow.

As a Marshall I saw another Marshall take an inmate and push his head into a toilet bowl because he asked permission to use the bathroom. When I brought what I believed was a wrongful action, to the attention of my Deputy Chief Marshall his response was: "You saw nothing, and remember you're still on probation." The same Marshal was working on the weekend, assigned to the cell section of the Court House. When I looked at him, I did a double take. On his right arm, he was wearing a Nazi arm band. He was also playing Nazi music so that the people in the cells could hear it and making himself and his arm band visible to them.

The "outside" Marshals did the evictions. Let's just say that when they emptied a place out for an eviction it was really empty; in fact, everything usually went with them.

I was asked if I wanted to serve with the outside marshals, it took about a half of a second for me to reply. No, thank you . . .

Frank Walters

"In the absence of justice, what is sovereignty but organized robbery? *Saint Augustine*

Exams are for dummies and Stealing Time

One would think that in the Court system that its employees would function largely on the honor system, since they were charged with on a daily basis of upholding and preserving the law, and keeping society at large safe from its criminals.

Wrong idea in this county system, it doesn't work that way at all.

Take exams for instance; it is quite common knowledge that staff positions in the Court House are graded with numbers. The higher the number is, the greater the pay.

Needless to say there was very stiff competition among the staff when it came to promotions. But, like so many other things at the Court, it was fixed; it was not a level playing field.

During the year, there was a regular series of exams which were announced well in advance. This gave applicants sufficient time to prepare. For some of us, this meant buying prep books and attending courses. The exams were offered for support clerical staff, court clerks, secretarial and of course court officers wishing to attain higher ranks.

There were those who looked anxious and worried until the results were posted. However, The Wizard of Court House Corruption, the power hungry Major bragged loudly and regularly that he had a close relative who would provide the answers to upcoming exams. Presumably there was a premium that was attached to this. The premium no doubt, involved cash, green, coin of the realm, in some large denominations.

Of course the Wizard's minions saw themselves being promoted regularly from staff officer to Lieutenant and so on. They were also promoted from staff officers to Court Clerks and so on and so on. They really knew how to work a system.

Thus the scallywags were able to perpetrate thievery of the worst order. The taxpayers of New York State ultimately paid the price and bear the burden of their treachery.

For although their promotions are undeserved; each year of active service in which they were promoted, saw a ten to fifteen percent bump up in their pay plus accorded benefits. The bitterest pill to swallow though, of course is the intentional padding of the pension, for these promotions produce very healthy pension incomes for life which can be transferred to another party after death.

Since these individuals rarely serve until full retirement age, they usually start collecting in their very early sixties and continue to collect for an average of fifteen years.

The average Joe, John Q. Public is getting it in the neck. We pay. We will keep on paying because the corruption goes unchecked; there are no guardians to stop them from their deviance. It is a small wonder that our real estate taxes in New York State and most particularly here on Long Island are on a never ending escalating climb. The exodus from our county is like that of the Great Depression with young people heading to the West and South in hopes of a better life. These thugs are part and parcel of this dilemma.

If this wasn't disgusting enough, they are even more creative about stealing from the taxpayers when it comes to moonlighting. Because Court Officers are Peace Officers and carry weapons that they occasionally discharge in the line of duty there are certain proscriptions on their business and employment activities, not unlike Police Officers and uniformed Firefighters. As such, they are prohibited from engaging in any business that sells or distributes open liquor, such as a bar or strip clubs. Although one Captain boasted about being a partner in at least two "Gentlemen's Clubs", but then again, he flew in the right circles.

One of the most common jobs, therefore for Court Officers other than seeking coveted overtime is working as a security guard. Court Officers are highly prized for their demeanors as they are usually much more calm than other uniformed officers most likely since they are not worn to the nubs from chasing criminals in the streets perhaps or possibly their exposure to such a range of crime inures them to petty criminals. They are also able to carry weapons and are seasoned at handling and detaining prisoners. Best of all, they don't work shifts so they are very reliable.

Enter the Wizard of Court House Corruption. It is well known that certain Courtrooms or Parts do not function much past two thirty in the afternoon. They have a very short calendar after lunch. In the old days, everyone, judge, court clerk, court reporter and officers were permitted to discreetly go home if their Part went down after lunch. After all, they had done their day's work.

The Office of Court Administration (OCA) does many things; one of their main functions in respect to the various Courts is oversight. As a part of ongoing fiscal management and oversight, OCA installed a time clock system called Chronos.

Each employee was given a swiping card to record their signing in and out of work. The Chronos machine electronically noted; similar to an ATM or bank entrance device, the exact time of your entrance and departure. Before this, we manually signed in and out. This honor system was very flawed as you could not be present for days on end, if someone was willing to sign you in and out and you had a posting that was out of the way, no one would know.

It was of course, a hard and fast rule that you were never permitted to touch or otherwise interfere or alter another employee's swiping card.

Now we are presented with a puzzling set of facts, maybe. The Wizard had a group of his cronies working as security guards at a baseball stadium in Queens. Somehow, some way as if by magic, they were able to drive from the Court House in Hempstead to the Ball Park through rush hour traffic and get there in less than twenty minutes.

No one could figure that one out. You see, they were due to start work at the stadium at five sharp. Our day at the Court House finished at four forty, now our parking lot alone was a mad house with all of the staff, clerks, officers and some of the judges leaving at the same time. We all had to line up to swipe our cards before we could even think about leaving. Must have been by magic, I guess.

The funniest thing is that we never saw those guys swiping their cards and somehow they always made it to the stadium on time and they didn't clock out early. One theory holds that someone maybe even the Wizard swiped their cards. Could it be? Oh yes, it could.

What's more an investigation by the District Attorney's office corroborated falsifying timekeeping documents in the manner mentioned. These actions were attributed to none other than the Wizard but because the powers that be needed him around for general skullduggery and he knows where too many skeletons are; the investigation has been repeatedly stalled until the Wizard retires. If that ever happens, we will see if they are investigated.

Once he does retire as that is a sooner than later eventuality, no doubt a new snake will slither in and take his place.

The thugs at the stadium have made quite a name for themselves. Aside from the normal security duties, they managed to embroil themselves in beatings and field riots on a number of occasions finding themselves the object of media scrutiny still, somehow they remain unscathed.

On at least two separate occasions, they were sued as a body for beating up paying customers who they felt had gotten out of line. One suit filed by two brothers had significant media coverage of two men swathed in bandages, badly bruised over much of their bodies, extremities covered in plaster casts, while they told of unbelievable horrors at the hands of a "mob" of security guards. Their suit was well regarded in the legal community and in the parlance was thought to have "legs".

Corruption reared its ugly head once again for somehow the suit was brought into Nassau County Supreme Court and dismissed without merit. These men were severely beaten, not just school yard roughed up, they were not playing for the cameras. Broken bones and significant work losses followed the incident for both men.

One of the other legal actions involved a married couple; this one may be settled out of court as the couple has the wherewithal to pursue the matter. They too, complained of unnecessary roughness at the hands of the guards. Their injuries were documented by visits to the Emergency Room.

Call them scoundrels, pirates, thugs or gangsters; they really should be called Untouchables. For that is what they have become; thieves, common criminals both in and out of the Court House.

By stealing an hour and a half of pay each day that this baseball team has a home game on a weekday; this occurs no less than fifty times a year. That is roughly the equivalent of two weeks' pay. They have been doing this for years. This is just one of their scams.

Because their thievery involves time records and the Chronos system if properly investigated, the perpetrators could face jail time. These lucky ducks never face accountability because they are protected by a wall of Wizardry.

In this scenario, the Wizard felt the heat rising. Having attained the second highest rank possible for a Court Officer, and having fattened his pension to his own level of satisfaction, it is just a matter of time before he knows that it's all over. Then he will return to civilian life and try to work his crooked magic in a new setting. For practice makes perfect especially when it comes to crime.

Frank Walters

"Ambition is a lust that is never quenched, but grows more inflamed and madder by enjoyment."
Thomas Otway

Badges for Sale

There are several ranks among Court Offices. This is not overtly obvious to the general public. There are the rank and file officers, the sergeants, lieutenants, captains majors and then the one and only Chief; the one man at the top.

When a man or woman first puts on a uniform and straps on a gun; thoughts of rank and promotion are not uppermost on their mind.

The atmosphere of the Court is frantic. And no one can take time away from the business at hand. There could be deadly consequences. So while dealing with the public, or defendants, in holding cell or in shackles, we are immersed in our duties.

There is of course down time, when we sit and shoot the breeze. In these moments, gossip is shared, jokes are exchanged. Every now and again, the conversation turns to the politics of rank.

In our fair county, we are more than top heavy with brass. There are seven Majors among the Court Officers and only four jurisdictional Court Hoses. Someone obviously added wrong. Why are there so many Majors drawing top pay at a time when OCA is asked to trim the fat annually?

You see, in our Court House, badges and ranks were sold like items on EBay.

The word was wide spread that five thousand dollars got you a Lieutenant's badge. Best yet, it didn't matter if you weren't a Sergeant. You were able to go from officer to Lieutenant at the drop of a dime or more precisely five large ones.

There was a certain Court Officer who was thrown off two police forces; one for brutality and the second one for lying about it. He found his way onto the court officer's ranks and within four years he was a Major and still is today.

These promotions mean better raises, better pensions and a host of other small and large benefits; the old maxim that rank has its privilege really does apply.

Now the price of the Lieutenant's badge was small when one considers the return on investment is no doubt in the neighborhood of five to one per annum. This could be greater depending upon the length of service.

I was personally approached by The Wizard of Court House Corruption and told to "buy" my rank and really thought that I was hearing wrong. No, I was told. How did I think that Officers, B, L and M become Lieutenants? They gave at the office. I felt physically sickened by this thought. I told him to stick the badge where the sun didn't shine as I didn't have the money. After that, he really loved me.

Officer "T" a union delegate, was approached, and was told to put five grand together and then the rest would be easy.

My head was spinning. I couldn't figure out why there was so much corruption and nobody seemed to give a hoot. Nobody did anything about it. No one policed it, no one tried to stop it. In fact, it was encouraged like a bumper crop of beefsteak tomatoes.

The fox was guarding the hen house. That is to say, that the District Attorney wasn't interested. He took a completely apolitical stand. He did not allow his employees to become involved politically. All the while, however, he took his marching orders from Party headquarters. His rule of thumb was to look the other way.

This was not only true when it came to the corruption that I witnessed; but anything to do with anyone political got fast tracked. Things were disposed of; no muss, no fuss.

The really burning question was what did the politicos have on the DA that kept him so tightly under control? Why was the saintly DA happy to allow such rampant corruption to continue unchecked and thereby grow in epic proportions?

The answer is simple; greed. There was an apparently convoluted financial benefit to the DA playing party politics. They let him keep his job. I often wonder how different things might have been if everyone did their jobs as they were supposed to do and the Court House was really a place for justice. What would that be like?

So, as a result, our Court House was stinking with Brass. Most of the rank and file members had to work two jobs in addition to their spouses' working to make ends meet. The idea of spending or even having a spare five thousand dollars around to buy a rank upward was a lollapalooza.

Personally, I took an officer's exam and scored high enough to receive the rank. The job, however, was given to someone else, on the grounds that he begged and cajoled the upper ranks for it. I scored twenty points higher than he did, but he whined until he prevailed. Gotta love it!

So many times over the years when guys or women got promotions, we always wondered how it was that they came about. Did they earn them or buy them?

It has become a little stricter now; you can't go directly from officer to Lieutenant. Maybe somebody decided to make some extra money.

Now I don't mean to say that all court officers, judges and employees of the system are corrupt, but the corruption touches everyone.

The really bad apples, like the Wizard of Court House Corruption are standouts, they wield so much influence and power that the judges are afraid of them. Their fellow officers have no choice but to bow down and play ball or suffer the consequences.

When there were consequences they were severe.

Frank Walters

"This is a court of law, young man, not a court of justice."
Oliver Wendell Holmes

Unequal Justice for All

In the penal code, few offenses stand out more than murder or acts of killing in any capacity.

The young mother sat with swollen, sunken eyes. She was not shackled at the ankles nor hand-cuffed, nor restrained in any manner.

As the judge took the bench; there was an exchange of familiarity that passed between them. The judge, the Administrator had a problem with Drink; but thankfully it was early in the day yet. So, as he held her paperwork, his hands trembled, longing for that first sip of the day, and I do not mean coffee.

The Courtroom had been cleared as a courtesy. There were only nine people present; the judge, the two court officers, he court reporter, the accused, Assistant District Attorney, accused's husband, and a distinguished looking older gentleman with an impressive head of salt and pepper hair. He had a bird like attitude of hyper-vigilance about his surroundings and the goings on.

Here, before the judge stood a killer. Her weapon; her late model car; her victim was a voiceless, blue collar laborer. That he was in his thirties, the father of three, and the sole support of his family did not seem to matter. He was crossing the street in a crosswalk. She was driving drunk.

Her blood alcohol level was well above the legal limit. She reeked of booze and cigarettes. We knew this well might not be the last time she would appear in a court room in this manner for such an offense. Although she spoke of remorse, one could tell that she was sorriest for herself and the fact that a night of partying ended badly. We that had consciences were sickened by this and many more cases such as this.

She never served any time, never did any community service. No, she didn't even get off on a technicality. She was given the "party" treatment. Her cousin was the reigning Executive Leader of a very active and productive area in southwestern Nassau County. It just happened that the Administrative judge and she lived in the same community. They were neighbors who attended the same church. Her only charge was a minor misdemeanor; she escaped by paying a fine. She retained her County job and made sure to buy her political tickets as both she and her husband were on the public's dime.

This scandal was mentioned only a few times over the years, when various folks would get off scot free on horrendous charges.

One that springs to mind is a story that was told to me by a judge that I had become friendly with. He always told me that this other guy was "tightly wrapped" and to watch out for him when I served in the county's criminal court rooms.

This solemn looking fellow also had been an Executive Leader, a member of the elite and had a really tight inside track as one of his best pals was oh so close to the Head Honcho. My judge friend had told me that this man, who had the look of a Post Office Wanted poster, would condemn court officers, clerks and reporters who dared to disagree with him; and that he obviously had anger management issues.

Little did we know, that his anger management issues, resulted in him burying a carving knife in his petite wife's back. Of course, Mrs. Judge did not press charges, and of course the poor troubled nice man did not go to jail like so many other assailants. He got counseling, and with the help of his fellow party members at every level returned to everyday life.

Judge D. meted out justice with a very firm hand. He was known to hand out harsh and regularly maximum sentences. But my heart grew very heavy when I learned that he too, had anger issues that he vented on his spouse. A dear friend related a story where the good judge and his wife met another judge and his wife for dinner. Mrs. D showed up with a cast on her arm and a swollen and bruised face. Describing herself as clumsy, my friend told me that the obvious conclusion was that he had beaten her "again". Mrs. D was overly embarrassed of her injuries and was not a clumsy person; however, she was injured often like an abused child.

The old maxim about power corrupting is certainly true because these two men felt that they were above the law. They may have felt remorse, but they were repeat offenders who were continually domineering and abusive to those around them because they thought they could get away from it.

Learning by example is something that the court personnel catch on to fairly quickly.

I can remember as if was yesterday, the shushed whispering in the back hallways as one of our own had been arrested on a DUI(driving while intoxicated) and was due to be arraigned.

Arraignment is a humiliating process, no less so than arrest. However, in this circumstance, the arrest was probably less demeaning as it was anonymous.

In an arraignment, defendants are brought before a judge. They are usually in a somewhat disheveled state; as they have been in police custody for a number of hours. Defendants are shackled at the feet and handcuffed sometimes at the waist or wrist in sets of two. Many of them for various reasons are wearing prison "orange" jumpsuits.

This arraignment was very different. It was held in a closed court room, with only the necessary people in attendance, and the defendant was accorded every courtesy. The result was the lightest possible charge and no jail time. What's more it was like he hit the lottery because he went on to serve as the Chief Clerk of that Court, now had he been convicted of felony DUI, or a serious charge, that promotion would have been impossible.

Are we seeing a trend here? It was a different kind of judicial system for insiders.

Money could get you just so far, political connections were the most valuable currency.

Justice was not blind; it was handed out like ice cream at a picnic. Anything at any price; one judge had a secretary who had prior arrests for solicitation as a prostitute. Her father was—you guessed it—politically connected to one of the most powerful leaders in the County. Now may I ask what kind of integrity does an individual such as that have? As secretary to a sitting judge, this person is privy to all manner of very sensitive legal documents and issues. If they would sell themselves, what would they do with unlimited access like that?

This position is a high grade on the Civil Service scale and is a very easy job if you have a decent judge. But, give me a break equal opportunity was never meant to include prostitutes! Because of her history, she had fertility issues; so on top of everything else, the New York State taxpayers were paying for her assistive fertility treatments.

Another secretary, although not a working girl; bragged about her bedroom skills and used her wiles to advance herself through the system. She recounted "breaking in" a certain Judge G's desk for him; she received two promotions in short succession.

The presiding Administrative Judge over all of the courts, a ruddy Irishman, used patronage as a personal dating service. It was well known that if a female attorney allowed him to advance around the bases; she would get appointed a guardianship, or a receivership, or whatever he could throw her way. Lawyers also knew the magic numbers to donate to his ever present campaign fund to get similar positions. The higher the number they gave, the greater the rewards.

He even went so far as to have his own "geisha" court officer that he affectionately nicknamed "Tinkerbelle"; she was his and his alone. Maybe she was light on her feet? She coincidentally retired when he retired.

The County's Surrogate seeking to overthrow a man entrenched in the job; ran on a platform of reform. This is because so much of that court's work revolves around guardianships, which are appointed short or long term jobs working for a single client under the court's supervision. These appointments often yield huge fees, so they can be plum rewards to people who helped the judges get them where they are.

Unfortunately though, he too, has to be called accountable; tending to appoint his own party members to these positions gaining juicy fees that reach into the thousands of dollars for the minimum amount of work.

Unfortunately just as to some much was given, to others, much was taken away.

Things like pensions, promotions, and jobs could be wrested away on a moment's notice if you didn't play for the right team.

But for the members of *that* team and let's say the team's Captains; life is sweet. Let's examine one such "leader". He was a lawyer, with a more than healthy practice; normal seeming family life and very greedy partners. Always wanting more and not knowing how to obtain it. The lazy man knows how of course; he steals it.

This wonderful scion of the party pocketed a cool million, didn't or couldn't pay it back, and never saw the inside of a court room or a jail cell. In fact after his foul deeds he went on to become President of a legalized gambling concern and although he was disbarred, faced no other punishment. Every year he raises a lot of money; is all cheesy smiles as he receives awards for his philanthropy. He's so smug he can probably pat himself on the back.

But why was he never prosecuted? To prosecute a case a few key elements have to come together One of these is a District Attorney willing to take a case and run with it. The sitting DA took his orders from the party boss when it came to matters of leadership and the inner circle. He would never have prosecuted one of the boss' pit bulls.

If he did, you could be sure that would be the last time his name would appear on a ballot. The boss always knows how to get someone's attention. Oh by the by, this thug who stole all the money; his partner is on the bench in one of the most senior capacities available.

In fact, the partner judge is the very same one that put the Wizard of Court House Corruption in power, knowingly. So, just in case you are thinking that this corruption is random and a byproduct of the system and perhaps even committed by a bunch of people getting carried away with themselves; think again. It's not. It's justice by design and by demand. Sort of like a pay per view movie where you know the ending; predictable, perhaps even dislikable.

They wield an enormous amount of power and they love it.

What is most reprehensible to me is that this is all at the taxpayer's expense.

B was a lifelong Republican. A favorite story of his was that he took a summer job between college years at a sleep away camp. This was the late fifties and much to his chagrin, the vast majority of the other counselors were liberals. He was thoroughly convinced that one was a card carrying member of the Communist Party after this pleasant enough guy revealed some ultra-left wing ideas to him around a camp fire.

These revelations piqued his paranoia to the point where he would not be alone with the "commie" again. So convinced was he, that politics lie in his future and if so, any hint of a pinko scandal could ruin him.

It was with this child—like confidence that B approached the world of politics. He worked very hard as a Committeeman for more than twenty years before he got his prize. He worked in several different capacities of Village government, prosecutor, Trustee, elected positions. Each time, the powers that be were testing the voter's appetite for his name and credentials. Saw his future in black robes on the bench. Then it happened; after securing a nomination and campaigning for five months, he was elected to the judiciary.

Unbeknownst to the political pack dogs, who thought he was an unknown, he had spent the greater part of his adult life preparing for this and had been immersed in a huge range of charitable, civic, and fraternal endeavors. From baseball to sick and dying children, he was there championing a good cause, sincerely because he believed you never should overlook the opportunity to do someone a favor. His charitable work found him on the national board of one of the nation's most well thought of children's charities today.

He loved campaigning, because he loved pressing the flesh and meeting people. To the politicos' surprise, everywhere he went, it seemed he knew people. He was thriving and loved the process.

When the votes were tallied, B, the unknown dark horse had garnered more votes than any other candidate; this is a field of a large number of judges. Some of his fellow candidates were actually running to succeed themselves and he got more votes than these incumbents.

Nobody was more surprised than B. He knew he had worked hard for his charities and other organizations; but he hardly expected the huge mandate that he received. What's more, every time he had an interesting case, *Newsday*, the regional newspaper ran a blurb on him.

His fellow judges were not happy. They chided and berated him in different ways, trying to unsettle him. One or two were supportive and friendly, they knew their fates were secure and had nothing to fear from him. The other two dozen acted like a rugby team in a scrum at a championship, always jockeying for position, a lot of pushing and shoving and growling.

Poor B, it got worse. He was a very good writer. He had been in a literary honor society in college and his secretary had been a judge's secretary before. She knew one way to advance was to publish, so she started to submit his decisions for publication. Add to this the fact that he was an excellent "law" man, meaning he really knew the law. As a result, before he knew it, he was getting his decisions published and the other judges were about to build a gallows!

As a point of fact, if a case merits interest or establishes a new aspect or precedent, there is good cause and likelihood that it will be published. So freshman Judge B had two decisions published in "the Law Journal"; and one that went on the books as new case law. So they figured out how to sink his ship.

One of his "buddies' told him that judges from the other part of the county had less competition and therefore got promoted more quickly from the other part of the county. This was the second time that he had heard this, and not in the same context so it made sense to him. The thing was, he was told that the way the county was moving politically, it would be very difficult for him in a few years' time in his area, so he needed to make a new alliance.

So of course, since this is coming from a friend, he listens. He uproots his family, moves to the other end of the county and incurs all sorts of political wrath as a result.

Now, he was pretty naïve to listen to his buddy, but "he had never steered him wrong before."

You see, in the judiciary, there is a pecking order, and most judges are elected preliminarily to the court of first jurisdiction. Then they are usually promoted to higher jurisdictional courts with longer terms and more money, prestige, etc. But as with everything in life; it is like a pyramid with a very few plum jobs at the top.

So here he was stranded in a part of the county that he really didn't know. His wife made friends more quickly trying to salvage things for him as she tried to weave them into the fabric of their new village.

His aim was simple, to advance to a higher court.

The machine and its' politicians toyed with him, draining him and his friends for five years, and over a hundred thousand dollars. Thousand dollar tickets were purchased and more were sold to others to rubber chicken dinners where speeches were broadcasted on televisions.

After the fifth year, they didn't advance him, he just ran to succeed himself in a race that they rigged for him to lose with no support from the very pigs that a year earlier were glad handing him for money.

The same machine and its henchmen that bled him and his supporters dry for thirty years turned their backs on him. They did nothing for him. He was set adrift.

One of his fellow judges tried to tell him not to be idealistic. "Don't think this is a meritocracy, because it's not; they will either give you something or they will let you hang around until they are done playing with you and then they won't."

The "they" referenced, is the Republican machine. Even though B had made contributions for thirty years and had brought many, many contributors to the party and even more money from his law firm, and even though he was a good trial judge with a great record; it didn't matter. He rarely if ever had a decision reversed on appeal. He lived for his job.

None of this counted for anything. Because the inmates are running the asylum that the Courts have become and they just don't care. They do things their way.

If they can't profit from an event, person, situation or thing, they will seek to remove it from their environment. So B ran for his seat again against a more than somewhat stacked deck. He didn't make it. Now it was re-invention time.

Back to private practice, traffic court hearings, disability hearings, serving as a Judicial Hearing Officer in as many as four counties, teaching college part time. He now had to work four times as hard to make a third less. This was all because he didn't follow the leader.

Remember that kid's game "We're following the leader, the leader, the leader . . ." In the arena of Nassau County politics, the leaders are Gods and all the rest of us are mere mortals. They taunt and tease and dispense patronage to a chosen few; usually their relatives or girlfriends. When you anger them, you are dead to them.

They killed B., them and his disillusionment. He died not long after losing his office. His idealism was so huge and his disappointment so great.

He felt he had failed and failed miserably at that. When he passed; the recipients of the big checks were not there as witnesses. His colleagues from the early days came and paid their respects and said what a great guy he was. His death and the demotion and destruction of others send out warning shots to anyone who might be an independent thinker—don't—think that is.

Just play the game, their game and you might get to finish. Keep your head and voice low and always speak well of the powers that be.

"The corruption of the best things gives rise to the worst."
David Hume

The Wizard of Court House Corruption

Money, influence and Power they have it all. They are the "In" crowd. The supervisors of the rank and file clerical workers, court reporters, maintenance workers, mail room staff even court officers and court clerks. The clique is alive and well and it rules with an iron fist.

Imagine mean high school bullies crossed with rotten bratty kids who always got their own way and that is the working atmosphere that one has to contend with on a day to day basis. You could be not the most physically attractive person who wears inappropriate clothing such as underwear hanging out or the lack thereof for all to see. But, if you're in with the crowd, then it's going to be a fine day for you today.

However, you could be the sweetest most competent, efficient, well liked person who the slug on the inside dislikes and what do you know, you get written up for something you didn't or wouldn't do.

What am I saying? You dared to breathe and show up for work? How could you?

You see, a very high percentage of the employees are political appointees. Meaning, their leader went to a meeting and asked for a job for their club and one of its members. It was known that there would be some jobs at the Court House. Voila! Take a test, pass, and you have a job, and a political obligation. In the good old days, you didn't even need to take a test.

But herein lays the rub. Once you are in the door, the leadership has shifted to something very dark and sinister. It is far worse than fraternity hazing, because at least there you know one day you will be an equal. Here people want to make you feel lowly about yourself hoping to make you feel more vulnerable and therefore compliant.

In the Court House, the Judges sit at the top of the heap. The Court Officers are unionized employees whose primary job is to protect the judge.

There have been hundreds of weapons seized and arrests made when citizens enter the Court House bearing weapons. It was a regular event to have the Court House cleared because of bomb threats long before the Uni-Bomber and Al-Qaeda.

So, as one can imagine, it is a tense atmosphere where fear and intimidation can allow a gang of henchmen to thrive and flourish. With so many people in crisis, feeling weakened and challenged, the bullies swagger in and start bossing the weaklings around. The sheeple; the majority of the Courtroom personnel are all too eager to follow. They fear if they don't they will be ridiculed, ostracized or even worse, eliminated.

The Wizard of Court House Corruption's power is absolute. If power corrupts as they say then absolute power corrupts absolutely.

A very shocking but not altogether surprising revelation came about some years ago when the OCA wanted to install digital automated court room reporting. Surprisingly, the judges and party leadership were demonstrably opposed; so of course there are still live court reporters. This is not shocking, what is shocking is that they want them around so that they can revise and rewrite; yes I said rewrite including omit, court proceeding transcripts to their liking. This allows a judge to find in favor of a certain party and then have the proof of his findings. Thus allows them to back themselves up with an altered transcript. This is so disgusting.

Surely, if someone appears in a courtroom seeking relief, and then the judge is only interested in covering themselves, we are not dispensing justice in a democracy. This is a system more reminiscent of Alice in Wonderland or Gulliver's Travels, capricious and whimsical with no reliable results, but here the fantasy never ends.

37

They just keep dreaming up more and more impossible situations for those they dislike and more plum positions and rewards for those on the inside.

The corruption festers like a huge boil, like a canker waiting to burst and it pervades the atmosphere. As a result, paranoia is endemic and arguments and fights burst out more often than in a normal workplace. Tension is thick and there is little relief.

In this atmosphere, evil takes hold and more often than not, wins. The common man has no clue what might be really going on as a kindly court officer directs him to a court room, is it a set up or is it legit, the odds are just about even. The court personnel who didn't play the game look like lost children with tired, vacant eyes always expecting the other shoe to drop, because it usually does.

So many times they have seen their friends and co-workers, humiliated and disciplined often for no more reason than sport. Or, because they believe that the individual or individuals pose some sort of a threat.

Two really fine civil servants in particular, to name just a few, were singled out and then excised, gotten rid of. Their stories follow.

These accounts sound more like something out of a totalitarian regime than a civil service union workplace; but even union delegates were not safe from the wrath of the of the Wizard and his cohorts.

The tide may get to turn as the pressure is mounting under the threat of a supposed investigation, or two. The Wizard of Courtroom Corruption cannot stand the light of day and as such, the rumor floats that he may soon be retiring.

I am not so easily convinced. I am hard pressed to believe that he stands to forego for one thing all of the extra income from "gratuities"; let alone the power. He has been on this power trip for far too many years now to "go gently into that good night".

"A surging, seething, murmuring crowd of beings that are human only in name, for to the eye and ear they seem naught but savage creatures, animated by vile passions and by the lust of vengeance and of hate."

Baroness Orczy

The Case of Officer "T"-the whistleblower who wasn't

One of the most famous books of all time was written by an Italian; its title simply, "The Prince". The author is very well known for his tutelage of would be schemers and plotters and his name Machiavelli, has been applied to people in a very unfavorable light when they manipulate, people, places, and things around them to their seemingly own betterment.

Well, enter the Wizard of Court House Corruption, who believes that an innocent Court Officer has reported him and some of his minions for their dastardly deeds. They had been stealing time for years, in epic proportions and they could be caught, some of the other officers were upset and rightly so, since falsifying timekeeping records at a State run facility is no laughing matter. The Wizard had it in for this guy anyway. That's the way it was, look at him the wrong way and that was it. He was just that powerful. He had this poor bastard in his sights.

When and if the truth would be told; it would turn out to be that a high ranking officer did blow a whistle. Someone did rat the Wizard and his gang of henchmen out for sneaking out early day after day, but it wasn't "T". The irony was that the Wizard told this officer to keep his eyes on everybody's time.

But by this point, a huge snowball of sorts started rolling down a great big hill called corruption. Many people played a part in this plot for it was Machiavellian indeed and it involved many players over many months.

To understand what happened, one must also understand what the Officer was thought to have done. The Wizard's henchmen very often skipped out early with his help. This was a known fact. OCA it was thought became curious about the timekeeping of some of the henchmen; it was then rumored that Officer T dropped a dime and called OCA lodging a complaint.

You see, T had been a union delegate, he was popular with his peers he wouldn't rat on anybody, a rat is not popular. It made no sense that they thought it was him. Maybe it was because he didn't play on the side of the Corruption team.

What they did to him was systematic and rivaled what the Nazi's did to the Jews. First they singled him out, and then they convinced others he was a threat. I remember the Nazi slogan "The Jews are bad luck", they blamed everything on the Jews and after a while it took hold. It was sort of the same thing. Convince everybody who basically liked the guy that he was either a whack job or no good and then set him up for a fall. Then they selectively enforced rules and regulations, seeking to find him in violation of accepted guidelines of job performance. Now remembering that he had been a union delegate, this was no mean feat.

They set the stage; the Wizard of Court House Corruption, informed the ranking officers that he was going to "F___k him no matter what". To T's credit, it took some time.

You see he is an affable Irishman, who melded well into the Court House. He was a fixture. He was always good for a laugh although his jokes were sometimes juvenile; they were never at someone else's expense.

He was very well liked among his peers, so much so, as was mentioned earlier he was elected to be a union delegate. This was a position that held sway with the Brass and power with the judges.

So how could it come to pass then, that less than a decade later, he was broken into bits? Like a man crucified for his own cause, one might say they even pushed him over the edge.

They set out to destroy him and so they did. This of course is corruption, but it is also unbridled evil.

His usual sunny demeanor started to shift under the pressure. Any given day he could appear calm, cool and collected; or upset and unruly—almost unhinged.

It was a well thought out process. A campaign if you will. How is it that these individuals proceeded to dismantle and dissemble a human being? They got into his psyche and undermined his thinking processes. They refuted every bit of truth he tried to bring forth.

His first infraction regarded the length of his hair—now it would seem that even if this was a problem that it would be easily correctable. His hair touched his collar! This pettiness speaks to the depths of their desperation to be able to pin or get something on him, and if you ever saw him, you would know that his hair mattered to him, so it was a very clever maneuver.

No one took this reprimand seriously as there were more than a few officers throughout the ranks who thought themselves like Samson and for whom a Barber was an anathema. Yet it took hold and gained momentum.

This was one for the Wizard's team. Remember just like baseball, three strikes and they call you out—for good.

T did not take this seriously at first, mainly because he was not the whistleblower.

We knew who that was, and it was one of the crowd who flew around the Wizard.

The guy even fessed up to the Wizard when he saw that he was gunning so furiously for T and told him that T did not do it. He was adamant, he said, I did it, he didn't. It didn't matter; the wheels were off the bus.

Was he surprised? Who knows? But more importantly, would he believe it? No, he refused to see it, he kept on after T.

His hatred for T ran so deep that it was too late; he wasn't going to drop the vendetta.

So T was posted to an outer lying Court House. This meant a further commute every day for him but this is when I was able to witness firsthand what they were trying to do to him. He was always on time, took appropriate breaks and lunch hours and left at the end of the day at the stated time.

The henchmen began coming around; now you must understand this was a thirty minute drive from their normal posting, trying to catch T doing something wrong.

After a few failed attempts at surveillance by supervisors dispatched by the Wizard, it appeared they might have caught him at something. He was exiting a bathroom after hearing all of the conversation in the courtroom, and in his haste, left the rest room without completely dressing.

It is important to note that the bathroom is located blindly directly behind the courtroom, so that T was unable to know what the commotion was. He responded to the noise by coming out of the bathroom as quickly as possible. As he exited, he of course had hiked up his gun strap to use the rest room; he had on along with his tie. He was written up for being out of uniform. Now as a very obvious point of fact, one cannot use a toilet with a gun slung around one's hips it would be both a very dangerous and silly thing to do. So the fact that the gun strap was higher than normal was a good thing, and the tie is a clip—on most times and takes all of two seconds to re-fasten. Perhaps even more telling is that T was on an authorized break although the Wizard had stated "there are no breaks in the Unified Court System.", which is actually against policy.

He as a matter of fact, was not even asked if he was on a break, it was just assumed that he was not. Strike two was landed. This was more than ridiculous, but the henchmen came prepared with a camera so as to catch him at something. If this wasn't a set up I don't know what was.

Knowing this was not even enough to take up a union action, they really put their pea brains to work.

Now when it came time to a hearing, they were erroneous in saying that I was present as I was actually on a trip many miles away from that Court

House. There is a legal concept called "false in uno false entero," meaning if someone, usually a witness lies about one thing they will lie about everything. So in many courtrooms, a judge or hearing officer will give an instruction when a witness' testimony is impugned, to ignore any and all of their testimony as false.

Needless to say, this didn't happen in T's case, although it should have, they admitted the lies into evidence.

For now, though let's go back to the events. They knew they had to do something dramatic, something that would paint him as erratic, unstable and a danger to himself and his fellow officers. They had him posted back to the main Court House. They could watch him up close now, as he found himself posted in an auxiliary parking lot.

The regular parking lots at a time in the past had been deemed unsafe. The neighborhood the Court House was located in had a history of car theft and some minor vandalism if court vehicles were left unattended; so there he was.

The incident they contrived was less than believable, as the two female officers would attest. He was accused of trying to maliciously and intentionally gunning the engine of his car with the intention of running down a Sergeant who was in a crosswalk. Officers would be asked to sign statements. There were two female officers in addition to the Sergeant, and they made statements.

The Wizard of Court House Corruption was unhappy with the statements. The one female officer was a hard case, she would not change her statement. The other was weaker and the Wizard had a Lieutenant work on her over and over again until he got the statement he wanted, the statement that he needed. It incriminated T, it said that he tried to run the Sergeant over, which was crazy. Finally, he had something he could hang him with.

And so it went. But you see the problem, here is that when you are a pensionable state employee and you are fired for cause . . . . oops! There goes your pension and benefits you worked so hard to attain. Court

Officers don't make a lot of money and they have to put up with a lot of different negative things in their everyday work.

They are regularly tested for tuberculosis if they have come in contact with an inmate who had the disease. They may have been spat upon, scratched or bitten by someone with HIV or AIDS. They get injured by inmates as a regular part of the job and court room incidents are not unusual. The scenes that are replayed on the media wherein a defendant goes wild in a courtroom happen with more frequency than anyone would care to admit. That is why there are metal detectors in Court Houses and there have been for many years; long before the threat of terrorism.

Talk about terrorism, T had his own private band of terrorists functioning around him and if he wasn't paranoid, he should have been. T was taunted terribly at this point, and it was going to get a whole lot worse.

They added one more charge on for T. After the alleged incident, when he returned to the Court House, he was asked to put his gun away, as there was going to be a meeting in a female Captain's office. T's gun locker key was in his car, a precaution; he decided he needed to take. Another officer, a minion of the Wizard of Court House Corruption, offered to store T's gun in another locker, T should have known better but he was understandably upset over the recent commotion.

Well, what do you know? After examining T's gun, it was found that he had non-regulation ammunition in it. Moreover, the ammunition they supposedly discovered was metal jacketed, therefore capable of tearing through the Court House walls. For general informational purposes, Court Officers are given ammunition, we don't buy it. We also don't waste money we don't have on designer bullets, as we rarely if ever have occasion to draw or fire our weapons. T swears that the bullets are not his, and since the chain of custody is highly flawed in this case my money is on T.

The kangaroo court was about to be in session and here was where the Wizard of Court House Corruption showed his mastery at destroying other people's lives.

Because of the serious nature of the charges; there had to be a hearing to determine what cause of action that they would do what they ultimately accomplished.

The charges were summarized as follows; two uniform infractions, repeated insubordination, failure to keep his weapon properly loaded, carrying impermissible ammunition, arriving late for work, and accelerating a car aimed at his supervisor while said supervisor was in a crosswalk.

The Wizard of Court House Corruption rubbed his hands in glee, because one thing the Office of Court Administration cannot abide in insubordination. They abhor it when anyone breaks the chain of command, Of course, this was known going in so that the verdict of the Hearing Officer would be a slam dunk.

They made their whipping boy an example for any that might follow. If you don't play ball with them you will be dealt with and dealt with severely.

T contacted the union, he knew the drill. Officers pay dues and part of the dues money goes to a legal fund. The union retains attorneys to represent its members; especially in employment scenarios. The union attorney was in contact with T and for some God forsaken reason made a unilateral decision that he could not represent him in this matter. They were banking on T not having the wherewithal to be able to retain an attorney, not so. Although it cost him the equivalent of three years' salary, he hired the biggest, bravest guy he could afford.

Now it must be remembered that the union attorney practices law in Nassau County; so the Wizard trumped T. Everybody knew that the Administrative Judge let the Wizard run the Court, so if the attorney went up against the Wizard, he could forget about his law practice. His documents might get lost after filing. He might not get notified about a change in court appearance date and times; basically they would mess with him until he had no livelihood. Just like they were trying to do to T; only T didn't see it coming and so far it was working.

T has friends so he was able to assemble character witnesses who spoke in his behalf. Also there was a division between the two female officers, the first one remained true to her statement as she originally wrote it; stating that T was nowhere near enough to hurt or harm anyone in any way. The other female had the doctored statement.

Perhaps even more telling though, was the appearance of collusion between OCA, in the form of the adjudicating hearing officer and the prosecutor. Every day there were friendly lunches and meetings over coffee during the disciplinary hearing. It looked like T didn't stand a chance. This was the equivalent of a sitting judge lunching with a DA or defense attorney that they are on trial with. It's just not done.

The Court painted a picture of an unreliable, irascible, mentally unstable wig nut. The Henchmen were lined up like penguins that all walked the same walk and talked the same talk. Yes, T was insubordinate; yes his gun had bad ammo in it; and on and on. I wondered how these people could sleep at night or what the Wizard of Corruption had on them that they were willing to sell their souls and trample on another man's.

This all felt like a bad dream, I waited to wake up, but it didn't happen. No matter what T's witnesses said, good fine Officers of long standing, they were ignored.

Nobody was listening. The drivel the Court was shoveling out was being swallowed hook, line and sinker. I was in awe. I had to hand it to them. They did a very thorough job. They did their homework and got to everybody.

I couldn't believe my ears. After so many years in the Court system, you get a feeling for how a trial or hearing is going. They really had nothing but hearsay evidence on him. And that was admissible!

It cranked on and on and as it did, T sank lower and lower in the chair until it looked like he would disappear entirely. I know that was the effect that was desired.

His attorney who does not like to lose was pissed. He could not believe what was happening. The hearsay thing had him nuts. With that admission he basically told T it was a ticket to allow them to tell any lie about you and say someone else said it without having to produce that someone. It just never happens, said he and I just don't get it.

T and I got it of course, because we worked with these thieves every day. Believe me when I say this was about robbery. They were robbing the State of time by leaving whenever they wanted and they wanted to punish someone for blowing a whistle so it might as well be T. They didn't like him much anyway and he was only rank and file, not Brass. He was not heavily politically connected. He got his job by taking a test; nobody put in a word for him.

They made T look like Jack Nicholson in "One Flew over the Cuckoo's Nest". He is anything but. He is a mature guy, who thinks his jokes are always funny; they're not and he will do anyone a favor if they ask.

By the time the dust settled, he was out of a job, a pension and his health benefits and $150,000. He had to pay from his own pocket for his defense. He is appealing now, and hopefully, because the Wizard has to retire at some point, and then who knows, T may at last prevail.

The worst of it of course is that this man is not in his thirties, for whom job offers are falling off trees. He is well into his middle age, when corporate America is closing its doors and retraining is rarely if ever an option.

The damage to him psychologically as well, is immeasurable for their onslaught was slow and measured as it was over a two year period.

Can you imagine how it would feel to be tortured on an everyday basis for two years?

The truth is bound to come out and when it does it just may have a different result. No one deserves to be raked over the coals as he was. There never was before nor has there since been a Court Officer treated in the manner T was.

He made history.

His case has set a very ugly precedent. The firing of a union Court Officer over a trumped up, make believe charge by a corrupt, evil fellow officer. It never happened before and it can never happen again just like the Nazi's. Remember I said that.

"I shall earnestly and persistently continue to urge all women to the practical recognition of the old Revolutionary maxim-resistance to tyranny is obedience to God."
Susan B. Anthony

When No meant no job—The case of "G"

While preparing to write about this terrible, tragic incident, I paced back and forth in my mind over and over again about how this woman will feel reading about what was done to her. But the actions taken against her were so grievously wrong that they must be included.

She was a loyal and devoted employee, a seasoned Court Reporter. She didn't fall into that questionable area of individuals that some would regard as strange or awkward socially in any way. She would never make it onto that cast of that hit sitcom about that office where everyone is weird because she simply is not.

One Supreme Court Justice in particular, who was extremely persnickety, loved her for her accuracy. She was an athlete; so she had a neat and trim figure.

Now to understand her plight, one must take a glimpse into the working conditions and environment of a court reporter. Firstly, they carry around a machine that has some weight to it; they bring this into the courtrooms where they do the public part of their jobs. When the live sessions are done, they then retire to their respective office quarters where they transcribe the shorthand notes produced by the mechanism into a readable 8 ½ by 11 normal document with all parties identified. It closely resembles the script of a play, except that is a very serious item.

So you can see that Court Reporters are therefore essential to the Court System. Digital recording has its limitations; although in places where it has been implemented one could argue transcripts should be more authentic.

The Court Reporters record every word during actual Court proceedings. An experienced Court Reporter knows which wise crack remarks to omit in the benefit of a judge; which grammatical errors to correct and which points to include. These may or may not have been on the record.

As their hands fly gracefully over the keys, they sit poised in front of the judge's bench, capturing every sound. They are extremely skilled to be able to type at the speed of human speech.

Depending upon workload, they may be producing many transcripts at once. This is because some trials and hearings are of short duration.

The reporters work in a large office area together. Ms. G functioned well in this atmosphere for more than twenty years. One would think that she had the hang of what she was doing.

Upon doing a simple internet search for Office of Court Administration disciplinary hearings; this accounting which will be dealt with within these pages pops up at the top of the search engines.

Why? Because of the true circumstances under which the termination occurred, all eyes were on the case. Everyone was wondering the same thing. How would the Office of Court Administration deal with this set of facts? They would obviously have to concoct a set of lies and exaggeration about job performance and the job history. Remember, this was a civil service job with a pension, union and no precedent.

Her supervisor, let's call him the Beast, ran with The Wizard of Court House Corruption. He was self-absorbed and half-witted at best. He lusted after her with a passion that was unreal.

Now in the Court House when you see the faces day after day; you take people and their habits for granted. After all, everyone is doing a very tough job, and in tough times, tough people pull together. That is how I learned it was supposed to be. Anyway, certain folks get known for the way they dress or their hairstyles, still others may stand out as cheapskates, so cheap they squeak. Early on others may stand above the crowd because they are so early they open the Court House, while others are running in the door at the last minute every day.

So it is that we got to know one another fairly well, and Ms. G was neither a liar nor a complainer. She worked with the best and the worst of the judges equally well and she knew her stuff.

But, all of a sudden, things changed. The Beast wanted her and he wasn't taking no for an answer.

This woman began her career at the Courts thinking that she was getting into a secure, stable situation. As a civil service employee, she felt protected by her union. She had certain rights or so she believed.

The Office of Court Administration is bug on human resources and training and development. They have spent many millions creating pamphlets and manuals on various employment topics. These materials are regularly distributed to supervisory personnel. There also are regular mandatory training sessions that supervisors are required to take. All of these issues concern employees' rights and benefits.

Topmost among these rights when it comes to women in the workplace of the court system is sexual equality, sexual discrimination and sexual harassment.

Every supervisor is trained and graded on how to even remove sexually charged language from their speech. In this way, they are able to avoid even the slightest hint of impropriety. They are schooled in how to avoid sexually questionable gestures toward other and same sex employees; and lastly, most importantly, they are rigidly informed and indoctrinated about what constitutes sexually harassing language or overtures both directly and indirectly. In this way, no one would become a victim by making unwitting stupid comments to a third party, for this too is harassment.

Supervisors have a guidebook, or pamphlet for their use that instructs them on, if and when language is inflammatory; and how to address other and same sex employees. They are told to refer to this reference tool when in doubt. They are also shown how to gender neutralize their language and thereby stay out of trouble.

Well, the Beast obviously ignored his instructions because he was like a hound at a fox hunt. He told anyone that would listen what he was going to do to that P___y if he got a hold of her and that he wanted her to s___ k his C___k.

These kinds of comments were repeated over and over again. Ms. G became concerned. She knew she couldn't outrun him forever. She tried and succeeded most of the time never to be alone with him which helped buy her some time.

You see, the more she resisted, the more of a challenge she became to this sick puppy. He was depraved, there was no doubt. But, at the Court House, there were a lot of people playing bed bingo, so I guess he thought monkey see, monkey do.

Only this girl was no monkey. She is however, extremely physically fit. She was known for her physical prowess and because of her stature and physical conditioning; his lust was out of control.

He must have her. To some men, a second woman is like an extra dessert and he wanted strawberry shortcake in the form of this court reporter or else.

But, eventually, the confrontation came. She said no. She had to.

What could he do? Little did she know that "no" meant that he was mounting a campaign to eliminate her from the workplace. Her saying "no" meant no job.

The sexual harassment now took an interesting turn. The Beast must have consulted with the Wizard of Court House Corruption and got permission to go after her, because what ensued is one for the record books.

After twenty plus years of excellent service, all of a sudden, Ms. G's job performance became questionable.

What she was accused of, smacks of a woman maligned trying to defend herself, but unfortunately for her, no one witnessed the groping or the lewd, lascivious, drooling the Beast displayed as he hovered over and around her. He was cagey and careful.

In the system it is said that transcripts are routinely altered. Do I know this for certain, I have been told. They are known to be edited thus possibly forcing a certain outcome, or a case to go a certain way. Judges have been known to comb transcripts looking for "errors" to avoid the basis of appeals down the road that might result in reversals and therefore hurt their record or chance for election to a higher bench.

If Ms. G had been accused of the alteration of transcripts, colluding with another party to somehow influence a particular outcome, or some other serious infraction, well then there might be grounds for discipline, or worse. Get rid of her.

But no, she willfully and knowingly did her job, and did it well.

She willfully and knowingly refused the advances of a slimy supervisor.

She willfully and knowingly refused to play with the corrupt majority running the Court House because she remembered a better time.

For this lapse of judgment on her part; she was brought up on the following charges; insubordination to her supervisors, (the Beast for not prostituting herself, well, yes); they got a mealy mouth, spineless wimp of a judge to say she mouthed off to him too so, also insubordinate there too. They said her transcripts were late, and that she was excessively absent.

Now with as much time as she had in the system, she could be gone for six months before she would be out of leave. But they wanted to get her.

They alleged that she disaffected the efficient running of the Court House. I never heard that a guy remaining horny could have that effect but; whatever.

Oh and by, the by, the union didn't help her. The Beast had been a delegate. He must have put more than a word in. Besides, no one goes up against a crony of the Wizard of Court House Corruption and wins.

She worked in the system for nearly half of her life and had to spend years trying to regain what she worked so hard to achieve. This was all because she wouldn't play horizontal rumba with the Beast.

When work turns into a hell hole like that it's time to summon an exorcist.

The agony continued for a year and a half more until she was terminated. Not one to give up, she appealed the decision and eventually won some relief. She did not regain her job, but did get some of her benefits and compensation. She was not made completely whole but she did receive acknowledgement of the wrongdoing and financial compensation commensurate with that injury.

Other victims of the corruption game have fared much, much worse.

"It is not the young people that degenerate; they are not spoiled till those of mature age are already sunk into corruption."
Charles de Montesque

Are There Any Decent Ones Left?

The following stories are not drawn from the supermarket tabloids and with little effort and some talent for searching, you could find out their actual identities.

Every word of what follows is true. This is how crazed and depraved some of our jurists became.

Judge G was no rocket scientist. He was a lawyer but actually made his living selling furniture or shoes before being elected to the bench. To say that he was a bit of an exhibitionist is being kind.

His time on the bench was not distinguished by any great nor monumental law decisions; this guy could barely hold the law books up to read them. He was far from stupid, he just didn't seem to be interested in the things that most of the judges were.

These guys were keenly competitive. They competed about women and cars, of course; but on a work level, they never stopped competing. They were in a veritable race to see who cleared the cases the fastest; who got through arraignments quicker. One guy loved to brag that he could arraign someone in under forty five seconds. Can you imagine the foolishness of bragging that you are able to decide somebody's fate quicker than the next guy?

There was some merit to this verbal jousting as OCA was in continual oversight of the judges' rates of calendar control and case clearance. But some of these lunkheads; yes you read right, really believed if they did a good job they would advance faster. Ha! They had a snowball's chance in hell of advancing on merit, however, money, influence and knowing who to get to, now that's another issue.

Back to Judge G. He first landed himself in the media by taking a shower in his backyard in the presence of some neighborhood kids. Yikes? I forgot to mention that he was nude at the time. When the police responded, he was indignant and annoyed and merely turned the garden hose on them.

This sort of self-destructive behavior, would be Judge G;'s undoing. Usually judges get taken down because of three things; bribery, case fixing and poor temperament or temper itself on the bench. But Judge G takes the cake; his story is like a bad chick flick on a woman's channel written by his wife. The title would be: Dedicated to a Fool. Judge G got involved with the mob and flaunted it.

The judge said he felt so frustrated and disturbed that he sought a fantasy life for distraction.

This judge; was not a genius on the bench but he had a very exalted opinion of himself as his website boasted various accomplishments. What he was; was a disturbed personality that took outrageous chances and laughed at the system that elevated him and desecrated the robes he loved to wear.

After the garden showering incident, do you think this man capable of judging let's say a flasher or some other deviant exhibitionist? One might think he would find sympathy with them and commiserate. He might even identify with the accused and not find anything wrong at all. Their lawyers of course would seek bench trials; that is trial held before the judge alone in the absence of a jury.

But despite this lewd and outrageous behavior, he managed somehow to remain on the bench. Naturally, his self-destructive impulses had to go into high gear.

His outrageous hi-jinx would ultimately bring him down in flames.

Through some unknown introduction or circumstance, he and his wife became friendly with another couple as couples will. Only the other twosome in this instance would be troubling for anyone on the law and order side of things.

The judge and his wife found themselves more and more in the other couple's company. They were having dinners with a known mobster and his wife at mob restaurants. Now to cast a benefit toward the judge was he aware of the friend's endeavors? At a point, he had to be because the places he was having dinner in, you don't go unless you know someone. The question begs, what did he hope to gain? This was a young man in his 80's feeling life had passed him by.

What ensued in the coming years was so outrageous; it will surely be a TV movie eventually.

Now, the mobster was old enough to be a father figure to Judge G, and no doubt a commanding figure, so that may have been the allure; but whatever the case, he took a slippery slide downhill and fast.

The friendship motored on for a number of years, probably three or four at least. Were it not for the judge's penchant for hanging out with the mobster and attending business meetings with him, he would most likely still be on the bench.

He came undone by running his mouth to an undercover FBI agent. He and his friend for some reason had a meeting to meet this person (agent) at a posh, local hotel. During the course of the dinner conversation, the agent was posing as an international criminal who was trafficking stolen diamonds.

This lit Judge G all up because as it happened, he then launched into a conversation with the agent about trafficking untaxed cigarettes and gasoline and using car sales to launder money. He further buried himself by asking the agent to help him find a buyer for some stolen gems he had.

As if this bragging wasn't enough, the Judge Wannabe gangster took his craziness further. He crossed the line between judging criminals and becoming one.

For some insane reason Judge G set up a second meeting with the agent, his friend did not attend. At this meeting, his brilliance hatched a plan; the agent was seeking help in laundering money. Of course, the Judge would help; he could use his campaign fund to launder the agents' funds. The agent would pose as a political consultant and fundraiser that way when Judge G wrote these big checks to him no one would think twice.

But then, he realized it might not pass the sniff test. Somewhere during the discussion his brain started to partially function when he realized that the deposit of all of this cash might raise some suspicion toward his campaign. His main concern though; was that other campaigns might seek the agent's help because he helped him raise so much money; needless to say he really wasn't thinking.

No worries, he was fast on his feet. He had a friend he would ask to help. Now how destructive was this man really that he not only was seeking to commit a crime but now he was recruiting others?

So he worked out a strategy, a restaurateur friend of his would launder the stolen diamond proceeds; the Judge's would receive a five hundred dollar finder's fee, plus fifteen percent. The Judge collected his fee. But, in the bargain, he got much more.

His meetings with the agent were videotaped. He was arrested, and eventually was sentenced to the minimum sentence for money laundering. This was surely not what he had in mind when he signed a copy of his book for the agent and endearingly wrote; "thanks for being my friend".

Oh, and by the way, Judge G was not part of the party machine, he was on the other side; so needless to say no one intervened to try and help him from imploding.

An even more colorful character inhabited the criminal courts prior to Judge G. Judge M was much like Attila the Hun in a black robe. He often showed little or no mercy to the accused that stood before him. His fall from grace did not involve any other characters but his own alter egos, some electronic, some telephonic. All of them were menacing and maniacal.

Many said that he was a gifted jurist. Some said he was tough but fair. Still others said that he seemed distant and brooding the majority of the time. The confusion with Judge M was that instead of thinking that he dispensed the law, he thought he was the law.

The Criminal Courts are a tragic intersection of crime and punishment. Troubled masses of human frailty flow in and out on a daily basis, most deeply in pain. So many of these lost souls are unemployed, underemployed, learning disabled, less fortunate, drug or alcohol dependent, co-dependent, in bad relationships and simply addicted to horrible behavior.

Many repeat offenders only know the penal system and will repeatedly offend to go back "home".

For Judge M work was a refuge and he created a shrine for himself in his chambers. A judge's office is referred to as his chambers, at the level of jurisdiction for Judge M, his chambers were well appointed on the level of a corporate Vice President in an old main line traditional company.

The judges always demonstrate some of their own personal taste and flair when decorating chambers, he was no different. He liked to do things big. In this case for some unknown reason he chose to showcase a dummy in a regulation flight suit. Maybe he didn't feel lonely that way.

Whatever it was, he was ordinary on the bench. He did not attend a flashy law school. He was no dummy. He was licensed in more than one state. An arch conservative, he was quick to render an opinion on politics to anyone and thought that the country was in sad shape with a liberal President at the helm.

The pissing contest that would be his undoing began in 1991. At first it was just verbal sparring with an egotistical attorney or two.

Truth be told, he was a shy, retiring individual, who probably did not belong on the Criminal bench. That world is a very harsh reality. Very few individuals can dispense on a daily basis; and deal with the tremendous torturous issues and remain unscathed. Remember, that if an individual is standing before one of these Judges, they probably have committed many crimes, possibly a gang member. They may be a robber, rapist or even a murderer. Even for the mildest of these souls it is very difficult for the power not to go to their heads.

Whatever happened to Judge M some say he was a little crazy to begin with, he went into such a downward spiral, it smacks of Hollywood.

There are those who would analyze his behavior as bipolar disorder or others as a borderline personality disorder or perhaps even dissociative disorder. Whichever it was, it was menacing and harrowing for at least one defense attorney and his family and in true Court system style took almost five years to unravel.

It is said that many a truth is spoken in jest, but for this jurist who began to believe that he was the law, he wasn't joking although he often said he was.

Any other individual would probably land themselves in jail or in a padded cell for a very long time for half of the shenanigans that Judge M pulled off.

Let's start with the fact that he is a conservative and the attorney he took aim at is probably an open minded moderate. They were both members of an association of criminal lawyers. The association invited a very famous civil rights attorney, the very poster child of liberalism, to speak at a function.

Judge M, for some unknown reason, took great umbrage at this and started a poison pen campaign, believing this defense attorney responsible for the choice.

The attorney is a scrapper, an intellect, who will not be pushed around. He responded good naturedly as naturally, a judge wields a lot of power and he is after all only an attorney.

But Judge M was not satisfied. He held a high rank in a militia like civilian force and perhaps that is where part of his God or Caesar complex came from. Perhaps it was the Court itself. Whatever, it was war and he was going to show that so and so exactly who was in charge.

So, when the attorney; who was popular among his peers, was elected to an office in the same association, the judge wrote a scathing, nasty letter about resigning and about the attorney's negative impact on the association. He further demanded that this horrific correspondence be shared with other influential attorneys. The attorney then thought the judge was coming after him. This was only the beginning.

Judge M turned up to a Bar Association function with a document written on judicial stationery openly criticizing this same attorney on many levels, and other attorneys as well. The letter also promised judicial retaliation for making unfounded complaints against judges. This function was a social gathering and this behavior was thought of as both bizarre and very mean spirited.

This was because the attorney wrote to the Administrative Judge to complain about Judge M. This was something that this attorney did all the time.

The other judges rolled with it and thought of it as a tactic he used to gain traction for possible appeals. They also believed this attorney to be possibly ant-Semitic since nearly all of his complaints, were directed against Jewish judges. This was ameliorated by the fact that the administrative judge was also Jewish. In truth, he was neither displaying a tactic, nor being ant-Semitic. He just felt that if he didn't stand up for himself, both he and his clients would suffer. Little did he know what was about to enfold.

As far as Judge M was concerned, this letter to his boss was the last straw and he was out to get this guy now, for real.

Many believe at this point when Judge M broke down with reality because the actions that follow are ridiculous at best.

The attorney began to receive anonymous correspondence of a threatening nature. The judge referred to him in one letter as "donkey terd".

The letters continued some had enclosures of snit-depressants. Not satisfied that he was gaining ground with the attorney, he turned to the internet and adopted an alter ego.

He carried a gun and wore it routinely on the bench. However, when he pulled it out and brandished it in his chambers in front of this very attorney, that he was known to dislike; and some stunned others, it was clear he was off the rails.

He even went so far as to send emails to the President; he disagreed with the President's policy toward Haiti and wanted him to know it.

Meanwhile, the alter ego, with an assumed name was busy sending threats out in cyberspace. Much has been written about this; but what about the amount of time it took away from his job for him to be a cyber-bully and author poisonous letters?

He harassed and menaced the attorney to the point where three years after the attorney's original letter of complaint to the judge's boss; Judge M was suspended with pay pending an investigation.

When the investigation was conducted, Judge M lied through his teeth.

The letters that the attorney received were akin to kidnap ransom notes and were all traced back to the judge. They included American flags, leprechauns and the Tasmanian devil, something more likely to be sent by an adolescent at war with a buddy; not a middle aged judge. But some of the content was not merely harassing but disturbing as the letters accused the attorney of child abuse and tax evasion. Some of the letters were mailed; others were sent by fax. Clearly there was no rational thought behind any of it.

Although he never admitted it, it was proven by time records and password log-ons, ip addresses, etc., that the judge also sent the emails.

Almost seven months after his paid suspension, he was removed from the bench; most of the charges were for lying and not the actual commission of harassment.

In an ordinary world, another man or woman might have been charged with some crimes for his behavior. People like Martha Stewart have gone to federal prison for lying about one thing.

Because this man was a political insider, he retained his New York license to practice law for another two years and his Florida law license until 2000, nine years after he began his assault on the attorney.

He has petitioned to be re-instated. One does not know if he has been rehabilitated or feels any guilt or responsibility for what went on. But while it all was happening; he brought forth a multi-million dollar lawsuit against the state which failed of course, indicating that he truly believed that he was in the right.

Another judge distinguished himself early on as a crackpot. He drove a car that gave the intentional appearance of a police cruiser including an added turning spot light. His vanity license plate gave the appearance as if he were a person of high ranking authority and importance. He filed a letter of intent for candidacy every year in the hopes of attending political functions, or so he thought. Let's call him Judge R.

He had a lot of experience with the law, but he was no shining star. His resume boasts of all of his accomplishments but actually he was a legend in his own mind.

The support staff of the court tolerated his arrogance. He had a cartoon-like expression most of the time that ranged from scowling to a circus like grin when he was trying to win points. But he reeked of a shady character that no mild mannerisms could disguise. Judge R was not a nice guy.

Justice is God's Idea

By the time he ascended to the full time bench, he was a very mature lawyer. Probably somewhere in his 60's he appeared much like that dislikeable uncle in everyone's family.

His fall from political power and prestige began even before he assumed the bench. He was a perennial candidate after a certain point. He loved to throw himself around and make verbal threats and jabs, thinking he was funny or witty. But he made a real boo-boo that could not be undone.

He was elected to the lower Court bench in 1996. A year prior, however, he ran unsuccessfully for the Supreme Court. Supreme Court nominations are announced in mid-August and are highly coveted as they encompass a massive fourteen year term and it is the top rung of the lower court, the highest achievable normally with a first election. This genius approached his county political party and somehow divined that his share of campaign expenses was going to run about ten thousand dollars.

Frankly, that's a bit light; campaigns cost a lot, with signage, bumper stickers, phone banks, etc. The average campaign runs about five times that number per county. This is especially true when our Supreme Court candidates cover large spans of physical space and they run in two counties with a combined population of over five million people.

Anyway, rather than making a general donation to his party, which is more than permissible, by law, in September, Judge R made out a personal check for what he considered to be his "share" of campaign expenses. This is a violation of judicial conduct. Judges are supposed to be as removed from the political process as possible. He could have had his wife make out a check or as stated earlier just make a check out and not earmark it. You see, even and probably most especially when judges are running for office they are held to judicial standards of ethics and conduct. Count one of judicial misconduct was against him even before he put on a robe.

This might have been forgiven if that had been his only problem. But to understand how judges are supposed to act; we must remember that they are considered political figures only while they are actively seeking office.

Therefore they are prohibited from taking part in any political activity; attending political clubs, dinners, fundraisers, etc. except when they are campaigning. This is in hopes of keeping a more impartial and even handed bench. I highly doubt that judges forget what party elected them once they go on the bench. But, you never know.

He still hadn't been elected yet, but he was a year later, and that did not cure his penchant for getting himself into trouble.

He assumed the full time bench in 1997; three years later while *not* running for office, he participated in a political phone ban on behalf of a legislative candidate. He did not identify himself to the callers, but encouraged them to vote for this candidate. He insisted he was only doing this to promote "good will" in the hope that his party would endorse him in the coming months for a Supreme Court nomination. This activity violated six rules of judicial conduct.

Three months after his phone bank caper, still hoping to garner good will, he attended another political function. This one was a candidate screening meeting. He himself was not being screened, nor was he scheduled to be interviewed. He decided to sit with the interview panel to offer his counsel. He actively interviewed the candidates, asking questions about how they would receive the endorsement of the party. This of course was a blatant violation of five rules of judicial conduct. Many of the candidates being screened knew him by name; which is ultimately what led to the disciplinary actions.

Last but not least, he was elected to the Supreme Court of the State of New York and assumed its bench in January of 2001. New Supreme Court Justices most often spend the majority of their time in matrimonial parts. So too, it was with Judge R. In April of that year, he signed a restraining order against one of the parties in a matrimonial action. This restraining order was later vacated by a higher court on appeal.

This can happen and it is often the case in matrimonial actions that a party will take out a restraining order to bar the other party from the marital dwelling or to keep a party away from seeing their children.

Well, Judge R didn't see it that way. He took it personally. Many judges don't like to see themselves reversed because it is a statistic that the courts keep track of and may give the appearance of an erroneous finding on the part of the jurist.

Knowing Judge R to be hands on, he didn't react well at all. When the petitioning attorney advised him that the order had been vacated, he told the lawyer that he would be on the bench for another eleven years. He also told him that he had a long memory and would remember the law firm, and it was a good thing that they did not practice matrimonial law.

When Judge R was finally held accountable for his actions three years later, even he admitted that his words could be construed as intimidating and could be constituted as a threat, thereby indicating bias against the lawyer and his firm should they appear before him in the future.

Now, it is important to note, that judges attend a judges school every year for two weeks where they are brought up to date on the latest in all aspects of juris prudence. This school also emphasizes judicial ethics, temperament and conduct, so that even if Judge R was not unfamiliar with any of the rules he broke, he just chose to ignore them.

For the record, many people have told this writer that he actually attended a great many more political activities, but because he was not disciplined for those, they were not mentioned.

For all of his crazy ways, Judge R was not removed from the bench only censured. This happened in June of 2003 and he was therefore able to retire; sort of the difference between an honorable discharge and a general discharge from the service. He got the equivalent of a general discharge.

Because Judge R's offenses were mostly self-inflicted, he went on in retirement from the bench to open a law practice and serve as a part time judge or Hearing Officer, in later years, most recently, he has retired to another state.

We need to be able to rely upon our judges; to look up to them as the last line between the criminals and lawlessness. They above all need good judgment.

These three could be called stooges for sure. But what is more remarkable is that there are about forty judges disciplined a year in New York State. Considering that there are sixty two counties that is not a lot of judges.

The sad thing is that these three all were carrying on in the same county at the same time. What is far worse though, is that these are the only three that got caught-so far.

"Where justice is denied, where poverty is enforced, where ignorance prevails, and where any one class is made to feel that society is an organized conspiracy to oppress, rob and degrade them, neither persons nor property will be safe"
Frederick Douglass

The Mighty Have Fallen

A plethora of corruption exists throughout New York's legal and political system. The following accounts are a true and factual recounting. This problem is not just in Nassau County and was highly organized in some other counties.

What we have are details of horrendously immoral acts of corruption by lawyers, judges, politicians and court system employees. Some of the acts date back to the late 1990's but in true legal fashion; the perpetrators were disciplined or prosecuted no more than two or three years ago at most.

Again, because all of these egotistical maniacs have families; only the necessary and pertinent details have been mentioned, no names, this in the interest of reform, not crucifixion of loved ones.

Whenever possible, a major media's report is mentioned so that should the reader have the interest or the time and curiosity, you may read further sordid details independently.

The lion share of the individuals mentioned herein are not known to me personally or on any sort of familiar basis unlike all of the other individuals mentioned throughout the remainder of this work. Yes, that is correct, I know each and every person I have mentioned and have been witness to nearly everything that you have read.

As to the individuals mentioned herein this accounting, more than because of the nature of the Court System and various functions, either myself or those close to me are acquainted with these individuals and therefore the facts in these cases. This is not tabloid journalism. This is recounting of the decomposition of democracy's keystone-justice!

The New York Post does not hide from controversy and in the mid 1980's would have headlines every day that would scream with scandals of one sort or another. It would seem that Watergate propelled us on a course of no-return when it comes to our government and its leaders. One of its most tantalizing tid-bits appeared in October 2005, when it claimed that a sitting Brooklyn Supreme Court Judge paid Democratic bosses $50,000 for his judgeship.

Now the Brooklyn DA has been very keen on putting an end to all of this. Insiders say none of it exists. They have to say that don't they?

This was not idle gossip. The meat of these articles (three in fact) came from more than one source who stated that parties had testified before a grand jury to this same set of allegations.

The Justice himself it was learned had testified before the grand jury panel. One may say where there is smoke there is fire. For the record, to bring a seated Justice of the Supreme Court or any citizen for that matter before a grand jury panel there has to be a smoking gun.

Ultimately, three years later, the newspaper subpoenaed nine sitting and former judges during the defense of a libel suit. These judges all reared from the same sordid soil.

In an interesting development, one of the main grand jury witnesses, (another Justice) left the bench on a medical leave; the heat was getting intense, no doubt. It is no coincidence that this Justice took the bench, the same year as the judge on the Post's hot seat.

Now, why may I ask is it so hard to connect the dots? It is the same Party Boss who it was alleged to have sold judgeships, was also an Assemblyman.

The Party boss gets indicted, for grand larceny no less. He is a New York State Assemblyman; he can be sentenced to six years; he gets one to three. He is ordered to return $10,000 that he strong armed off of a judicial candidate. He thanks God and his family as he goes off to jail. But in true TV style he gets a last minute reprieve from a former Republican

Executive Leader who is now a seated Appellate Judge, his sentence was stayed pending appeal.

His web of corruption was a web of steel and it was legendary, you didn't get a judgeship, and you didn't get elected unless you paid the piper.

There was one man, an African American, educated on the GI Bill, quite a maverick. He was elected to the bench in Brooklyn in the 80's without any help. He called himself the Kung Fu judge. He owned a string of movie theaters and a lot of property. He died penniless in an assisted living facility after some crooked cronies got a hold of his money through a forced guardianship. It would have been cheaper if he had bought the judgeship. But they got him one way or another.

A Suffolk County Family Court judge obviously needed counseling as he found himself transferred after mishandling a child custody case very badly. One can only wonder what this judge was thinking to allow a father who had been convicted of possession of child pornography and third degree rape of a child to have overnight visitations with his three minor children supervised by elderly parents. What was his incentive in this matter?

He has been re-assigned to civil court.

The head of the state Independence party long the flag wavers for anti-corruption got embroiled in a bit of a sticky wicket over an improper $10,000 loan. It seems that the party chief's wife accepted a loan from a candidate for her company. Actually days after the loan was made, he got the party's endorsement. These are the same folks who were up to their eyeballs with Mayor Bloomberg over lots of money that he steered their way, so much so that one of his aides started helping himself to a cool million and now is wearing prison orange.

If you ask three paralegals and nurses if their bosses, lawyers and doctors are cheap; the majority will say resoundingly yes.

This is most likely due to the fact that they both have large business overhead with staff salaries, rent, insurance, and other usually expensive equipment to pay for. But most of the lawyers I know envy doctors. In some cases, in a lot of cases actually, master craftsmen lawyers actually earn much more per hour than doctors. Emergency room physicians are not huge earners. Surgeons however, earn huge sums-millions or multi-millions annually. There is one huge difference in the way they go about their practices—the schmoozing.

Doctors with established practices don't have to schmooze anybody unless they want a book or a TV deal. Drug companies until recently were in the regular course of business, accustomed to giving doctors trips and huge stockpiles of free pharmaceuticals in the hopes of encouraging them to prescribe their offerings to their patients.

For lawyers it is a different story; especially trial lawyers. They find themselves at the mercy of three disparate groups of people—their clients, their respective Bar Associations and last but surely most formidable—the judiciary. Other than a jury, judges can and do make or break a trial lawyer's career.

There are good lawyers and bad lawyers. The Journal News and Newsday have both reported that a prominent New York lawyer pleaded guilty to charges of public corruption in connection with paying bribes to a Westchester Councilwoman. He also pled guilty to a tax charge and faces up to forty five years in prison. Since his plea, he has decided to cooperate with the US attorney's office so his sentencing has been delayed. Two other defendants, the councilwoman and the city party boss accused of paying $16,000 in bribes have both pled not guilty.

The case of an Albany based Supreme Court Justice is really disturbing. This man was at one time a Catholic seminarian so one would think that the truth and ethics had meaning to him.

If you know court venues, then you understand that Supreme Court Justices sit on a wide variety of cases as The New York Law Journal reported in this case, this judge sat on a trial that saw a certain lawyer recover a one million dollar fee. That's correct. That was the law firm's fee. Now judges earn about $140,000 a year. So this fee made this judge's mouth water. He wanted at taste; so much so that he hit the lawyer up (on the phone) for $10,000. Now this is a big no-no. If it was a campaign year and it was a contribution; one might say that he had a big set. But no-it was for hold on—his legal defense fund.

Why would a judge need a legal defense fund? Well you see his judgment was always a bit eschewed. He had the lack of wisdom to buy about $2,000 worth of drinks for some lawyers by distributing $5 free drink coupons at a function. He also accepted the district attorney elect as a client in his law practice even though he presided over cases brought forward by the district attorney. The first instance demonstrates a lack of judgment, the second, misconduct and a conflict of interest.

Because of these incidents, he had allegations to answer to and charges to defend hence his legal defense fund. But his methods were more than questionable. No matter what, one does not ask a lawyer before your bench for a huge contribution.

This Bozo really blew it now. You do remember what I said about lawyers being cheap? Most likely the judge thought what's ten grand compared to one million?

Whatever he thought or didn't think, he had the non-presence of mind to up the ante when he organized a luncheon for a bunch of lawyers and invited another sitting judge, a surrogate. He excused himself at a point and had an associate lean on the lawyers at the table in his absence. The other judge refused to rat on him which resulted in that judge being censured.

By the time the fat lady sang in this little drama, the judge was removed from the bench and had a much larger legal bill than he would have if he didn't go lunching or dialing for dollars. His career was flushed over twelve thousand dollars and some free drinks for some lawyers. How is that worth it?

The fact that this attorney came forward and spoke up is highly unusual. The vast majority pays up and says nothing. They consider the money given to judges and their "associates" a normal part of doing business.

These expenses are allocated no differently than a travel and entertainment budget. One law firm I know of throws the most elaborate Super Bowl catered party where they give away huge prizes and it is akin to a wedding, lots of judges are there.

This judge lacked discretion, but one stands out for all time.

The New York Times was not alone when it reported about the judge who helped a robbery suspect escape by leading through a back door of the Court House. She was removed from the bench.

Now there is a movement afoot to reverse the paying for verdict and guardianship trend among lawyers. New York attorneys are urging revision in campaign rules, specifically barring judges from sitting on cases involving firms or attorneys that have contributed $2500 or more to their campaigns. In New York City last year, a firm actually lent a judge seeking office a significant portion of her campaign fund, knowing that she would be unopposed. However, there were still political fees she must "pay".

The tyrannical monarch she paid her fees to eventually went to jail on the same day that the Supreme Court justice who brought him down went too. Two unbelievably powerful scions of society now relegated to six by eight cells. One man is a scholarly gentlemen in his sixties, the other a nattily dressed sharpie in his fifties, both forlorn and off to do their time. They will emerge in a few years, a bit sallow and sunken, saddened by the experience. But will they have learned?

Will a new Party Boss emerge in his place?

New York State requires financial disclosure documents to be filled out by judges and politicians but only after they are elected. Perhaps they should fill them out as candidates and be blind to the election process in so far as money is concerned. Something has to happen to remove them from the mix so that they may function on a higher and less political level.

Most of these men and women are good public servants. But, if the Party Bosses pull them into a swamp of graft and corruption then our system of justice is doomed. We must fight to keep our judges above the fray.

Frank Walters

"There is no crueler tyranny than one which is perpetrated under the shield of law and in the name of justice."
Thomas Jefferson

The structure of the courts and how they function

Whether it's rural upstate New York or one of New York City's five boroughs, the structure of the courts of lower jurisdiction in New York State are basically the same. The most local or smallest courts one can encounter are village or town courts adjudicated by part time judges known as magistrates.

In different parts of the state, these positions are either appointed or elected. These courts deal with traffic infractions, parking tickets, and all manner of other village violations. These judges are very often politically active well-known local attorneys.

The next level of jurisdictional justice is either usually a Civil Court or a District Court depending upon locality. These courts in the first instance deal with all civil matters on the most basic level; landlord and tenant disputes; small claims actions, and civil suits with limits not exceeding $25,000.

In the case of District Courts, they deal with all of the matters of the Civil Courts and some Criminal matters as well. That is, they perform arraignments; wherein all those accused of a crime are first presented in court before a judge and also deal with misdemeanor trials. The judges are able to sentence defendants to no more than a year in jail.

The next level of jurisdiction in most counties involves the Criminal, Family and Surrogate's Courts. The Criminal Courts deal with those accused of criminal offenses. The Family Court deals with a wide range of legal issues, adoption, child custody, juvenile offenders, and many others.

The Surrogate deals with largely trusts and estates of deceased parties, special guardianships and other related matters as well fall under this Court's purview.

The Supreme Court deals with all contractual and civil matters, matrimonial, negligence, torts, malpractice, nearly any civil suit that you can think of in the first instance would be instituted here.

The Court of Claims deals with litigations taken up against the State of New York.

Court of Appeals and Appellate Division-Courts of highest relief wherein litigants appeal decisions rendered in lower courts, courts consist of panels of justices in some cases.

"Justice is a temporary thing that must at last come to an end, but the conscience is eternal and will never die."
Martin Luther

The state of the Court System Today

The victims of unethical and corrupt lawyers, judges, and employees of the state and federal judiciary demand accountability from those who abuse the power of the office while they remain absolutely immune". Kill all the lawyers.com

There is one word for the state of the court system today—deplorable.

The internet is jammed with websites decrying its rampant corruption, it would take days to define and list all of the current indiscretions.

There are sixty two counties in New York State and policies on the judiciary vary from county to county. But, of one thing you can be sure, the golden rule is alive and well; that is thems that has the gold rules.

A fun exercise might be to do some internet research on the cost of a judgeship. I did and found many citations that made note of the New York City ditty that went fifty thousand for a lower court seat and one hundred thousand got you the best seat in the Court House. All of the cases mentioned in the prior chapter speak to this. What is that old saying about if it walks like a duck and quacks like a duck?

The greatest injury from all of this of course is to society for if someone pays their way onto the bench, how can they dispense justice?

Of course with isolated prosecutions nothing can be proven, one bad apple and all that. But when the party boss in two downstate counties have both done time for basically racketeering where does that leave us when these are the men that pick the judges?

We can look at cyberspace and its myriad of allegations and it means nothing. But to be more specific about the state of the court system, the epi-center is the judges, so to analyze the court system, and its general condition; we need to look at who sits on the bench and how they behave.

So many judges seem to act as if a judgeship is a free pass out of civility. So let's throw out a few tid-bits about a few not so good judges. All of the judges mentioned sit on the bench in Nassau or Suffolk County, NY.

How does a judge afford a rare antique and classic car collection and put two children through college on a judge's salary? No his wife is not a trust fund baby. Creative accounting must be the answer. Oh I forgot to mention; his partner was the man who was not prosecuted but found to have stolen at least a million dollars from people's estates. The question begs how much was stolen that was not discovered?

One female judge got her judge's robes on knee pads provided by a former top county executive, she purred when he called, and this married woman lovingly referred to him as her "special friend".

One clerk had a running oral fixation with a judge so ugly she probably never looked up; but she was promoted and retired with a great pension.

One higher Court judge bragged that his Dad set up his judgeship with his bar mitzvah money. As he was from a north shore community, it was probably quite a hefty sum.

One political leader, now long since passed, was known as the patron saint of judges because he had an "in" with the party boss. No one knew if the "in" involved cash or just getting out the votes, but more judges got elected from his club than any other.

One lower court judge, after having heard of another's exploits, tried to break in every new secretary within two hundred yards over his desk. His second venue was a local hot sheet house. Of course he was happily married, right up until the Lord called him home.

There is a judge that is related to a leader, so he has hop scotched through the Court Houses up the ladder like a kid on a pogo stick. This man does not have a world of legal experience outside the system, and is not the most master craftsman inside the system either. But in a horse race, bloodlines always matter, and judicial appointments and elections are rarified horse races to be sure. This judge by the way is a prince, but patronage has really done right by him.

In an age where consumer accountability is at an all-time high, recommendations are being forwarded that we go easier on our judges. I think not. There are many fine men and women on the bench, but the better they are, the more they are offended by the rotten apples.

In January of 2011, the New York Lawyers Association, a group with 77,000 members made sweeping recommendations that if implemented would greatly weaken the judicial review process and ultimately compromise the integrity of our judiciary.

Just last year, a former Justice of the Supreme Court from the Bronx and his paralegal were found guilty of multiple counts of fraud, pursuant to an immigration fraud mill operation.

For more than eight years, they filed fraudulent amnesty applications and charged clients thousands of dollars in excessive filing fees. The paralegal was also found guilty of witness tampering.

He originally was removed from the bench for making lewd and lascivious comments to a female intern. He should have had a legal team like Bill Clinton's he might have fared better.

In all seriousness, making the review process easier for this judge could have possibly meant even greater trouble for him down the line.

A very flamboyant and well known matrimonial attorney was recently suspended from the practice of law for continual retainer violations, such as inadequate billing, and inadequate supervision of lawyers and paralegals under his supervision. This guy at one time was a superstar. The money involved in this case is paltry.

Hopefully, he will straighten this out. He can be arrogant, boastful and prideful, but he is far from the worst of the bunch. He also won some great verdicts for his clients.

The Police Crime Lab of Nassau County was deemed unreliable after it was revealed it was giving inaccurate measurements in drug cases. The repercussions of this are mind boggling. The greatest pity of course is that the good guys have to be perfect to catch the bad guys and a hole like this can let a lot of bad seeds wash through. Defense attorneys love technicalities and while the police could have a defendant dead to right if the evidence is marred, they have a problem. It would seem in this particular case that although some police brass were aware of some irregularities, they were powerless to correct it.

A whistleblower who worked for the state, let's call her CA is all over the World Wide Web, now rallying support. But, more than one of the state officials that she took on has decided to retire. I wonder why? She relates horrific stories, how she was subject to constant harassment, of witness tampering, and in summary making the trial sound like something out of a mob movie rather than a proceeding against a vastly powerful legal organization by an individual.

A horrific trend in dirty landlord/tenant cases involves the less fortunate. Recent reports out of New York City housing court indicate that landlords will go to almost any length to re-take rent-controlled and rent-stabilized units. They are actually toying with the elderly disabled and elderly disabled veterans. Housing court judges it seems are easy pickings. The case I researched, the landlord failed to issue the tenant a lease every year for the six years he was in the apartment, thus he was guessing the amount of rent he owed. The landlord tried to bring a competency hearing against the gentleman, because of his disability. Maybe someone should tell him that leg bone is not connected to the head bone.

The IVIEWIT Technologies lawsuit is a twelve trillion dollar case. The judges' names that have been suggestively involved with the case read like a judicial Who's Who. And by the way, that is involved, not in a good way. In the interest of an ongoing RICO investigation by the federal government, it would be imprudent to list any names, but a simple internet search will garner pages of entertaining results.

In Westchester County, it is alleged, that judicial records were systematically destroyed thereby denying the public access to them. There is an ongoing Federal probe aimed at the Westchester judiciary for some well-known problems or issues. It has been suggested that some senior members of the bench, one or two in particular, have been implicated under suspicion of verdict and trial fixing. So much so, that the whole county court system is under a microscope.

A former Administrative judge from the five boroughs of New York City fled to private practice when rumors started to circulate about an investigation and it was clear that the party would be over. A Manhattan judge was reported in the "New York Post" as having lied on his mortgage documents. He has not denied the allegations. He misstated that a Brooklyn residence on which he gained financing was his primary residence; he also resides in a rent stabilized apartment in the Bronx that he has stated is his primary residence (a condition for rent control). The same man seems to believe in hiring from within; since he hired his ex-wife, his secretary's brother, his executive assistant's nephew and the son of a court officer who formerly was his driver. Sadly for him; they were not hired for their experience; it was blatant nepotism.

A former Chief Clerk of an upstate county Family Court is suing her Administrative Judges on allegations she was forced from her job. The suit in federal court outlines a pattern that indicates a hostile and perhaps even unsafe work atmosphere was created and she was put in harm's way.

She was encouraged. It seems by the judge and his former Executive Assistant to spy on and dig up possible scandalous information about a Supreme Court candidate who was a currently seated Family Court Judge.

She was resistant at first. When she refused to participate; they started to make her life miserable. She was asked to substitute for other clerks in remote areas, if she questioned an order; she was asked about her loyalty and team spirit.

They dogged her until she couldn't take it anymore.

The biggest fish sit at the top of the pyramid serving in administrative capacities. Some of these jurists, have not been in courtrooms that much as they are excellent bureaucrats, who function best on and with paper.

There are probes ongoing involving all levels of the state's judiciary and it would seem that no one is safe. No one is exempt. Rocks are being overturned everywhere. One probe involves a dubious appointment of a sitting high ranking administrative judge to be a co-executor on a forty million dollar estate. This appointment involved a newly created will when the maker had been in a vegetative state curled into a fetal position. Many would be hard-pressed to believe that this was legit.

Now, sitting judges are not supposed to practice law, they may teach it. They may write and do other non-political things. In this situation, the judge needed a waiver to be able to practice law on this case. You see, by serving as a co-executor, he could bill and collect a handsome fee based upon the size of the estate. Now, remember we're talking forty million dollars of an estate.

It is questionable at best, that a supervising administrative judge, even higher ranking than this Administrative judge; would give this judge permission in a situation such as this. This was not a relation of kinship; there was a purported friendship which on the surface according to various media accounts is dubious, since the decedent was so addled for so long. These people were not his family. He alleged that he and the decedent were friends for thirty six years yet the lines don't seem to connect and the decendent basically drooled for the last three years of his life.

How can justice become so convoluted? How can men so misunderstand the words.

87

Every day when I entered the County Court House I saw those words . . .

"Justice is God's Idea and Man's Ideal"

This is what we aspire to, what our mandate is but who will answer for these charges of villainy and corruption?

"Justice, sir is the great interest of man on earth. It is the ligament which holds civilized beings and civilized nations together."
Daniel Webster

Afterword

Although we know the Court system is mired with problems and laden with inefficiency, no amount of whining or complaining will change anything.

Apathy has brought us to where we are and that is at the crossroads on the highway to destruction.

This is our Court System, a dynamic, organic organization that can and will respond to change. But we must demand it. It may appear to be sickened and weak; but there is hope.

The first step in treating any disease is the discovery of it. The second is determining exactly how bad it is and lastly, of course determining a course of treatment in hopes of a cure.

This is the only approach that can possibly work with the Court System. Any governmental institution is always a reflection of the society and civilization which it serves.

A corrupt and weakened Court System serves no one. We know there is a lack of faith in the system based upon the number of people who prefer to have their cases adjudicated on television. It is not merely the aspect of their fifteen minutes of fame. Many interviewed feel that in such a public setting, they will get a fair trial and that they will have their day in court, not only on TV. For every case we see, there are ten or twenty that are taped but never air, these folks still seem satisfied with their outcomes.

By demanding accountability and becoming educated to the legal process, the judges, the lawyers and others who inhabit the hallowed halls of justice will be forced to remember that they are the servants of the public and must serve for the public good.

Unless we demand honesty and integrity, we will not get it.

The truth has a life of its own and it is vital and vibrant. It is powerful and illuminating and breathes life into hollow spaces for as it has been said so eloquently and well . . .

The Truth shall set us free!